MANHATTAN PREP

Critical Reasoning

GMAT® Strategy Guide

This unique guide illustrates how to deconstruct arguments using a four-step process designed to build speed and improve accuracy. Understanding the underlying structure of arguments and answer choices is the key to quick reading and accurate analysis.

guide **6**

Critical Reasoning GMAT Strategy Guide, Sixth Edition

10-digit International Standard Book Number: 1-941234-01-1
13-digit International Standard Book Number: 978-1-941234-01-3
eISBN: 978-1-941234-22-8

Note: *GMAT, Graduate Management Admission Test, Graduate Management Admission
Council,* and *GMAC* are all registered trademarks of the Graduate Management Admission
Council, which neither sponsors nor is affiliated in any way with this product.

Layout Design: Dan McNaney and Cathy Huang
Cover Design: Dan McNaney and Frank Callaghan
Cover Photography: Amy Pierce

SUSTAINABLE FORESTRY INITIATIVE   Certified Sourcing
www.sfiprogram.org
SFI-00756

GMAT® STRATEGY GUIDES

0   GMAT Roadmap

1   Fractions, Decimals, & Percents

2   Algebra

3   Word Problems

4   Geometry

5   Number Properties

6   Critical Reasoning

7   Reading Comprehension

8   Sentence Correction

9   Integrated Reasoning & Essay

STRATEGY GUIDE SUPPLEMENTS

Math

GMAT Foundations of Math

GMAT Advanced Quant

Verbal

GMAT Foundations of Verbal

MANHATTAN
PREP

December 2nd, 2014

Dear Student,

Thank you for picking up a copy of *Critical Reasoning*. I hope this book gives you just the guidance you need to get the most out of your GMAT studies.

A great number of people were involved in the creation of the book you are holding. First and foremost is Zeke Vanderhoek, the founder of Manhattan Prep. Zeke was a lone tutor in New York City when he started the company in 2000. Now, well over a decade later, the company contributes to the successes of thousands of students around the globe every year.

Our Manhattan Prep Strategy Guides are based on the continuing experiences of our instructors and students. The overall vision of the 6th Edition GMAT guides was developed by Stacey Koprince, Whitney Garner, and Dave Mahler over the course of many months; Stacey and Dave then led the execution of that vision as the primary author and editor, respectively, of this book. Numerous other instructors made contributions large and small, but I'd like to send particular thanks to Josh Braslow, Kim Cabot, Dmitry Farber, Ian Jorgeson, Ron Purewal, Emily Meredith Sledge, and Ryan Starr. Dan McNaney and Cathy Huang provided design and layout expertise as Dan managed book production, while Liz Krisher made sure that all the moving pieces, both inside and outside of our company, came together at just the right time. Finally, we are indebted to all of the Manhattan Prep students who have given us feedback over the years. This book wouldn't be half of what it is without your voice.

At Manhattan Prep, we aspire to provide the best instructors and resources possible, and we hope that you will find our commitment manifest in this book. We strive to keep our books free of errors, but if you think we've goofed, please post to manhattanprep.com/GMAT/errata. If you have any questions or comments in general, please email our Student Services team at gmat@manhattanprep.com. Or give us a shout at 212-721-7400 (or 800-576-4628 in the U.S. or Canada). I look forward to hearing from you.

Thanks again, and best of luck preparing for the GMAT!

Sincerely,

Chris Ryan
Vice President of Academics
Manhattan Prep

HOW TO ACCESS YOUR ONLINE RESOURCES

IF YOU ARE A REGISTERED MANHATTAN PREP STUDENT

and have received this book as part of your course materials, you have AUTOMATIC access to ALL of our online resources. This includes all practice exams, question banks, and online updates to this book. To access these resources, follow the instructions in the Welcome Guide provided to you at the start of your program. Do NOT follow the instructions below.

IF YOU PURCHASED THIS BOOK FROM MANHATTANPREP.COM OR AT ONE OF OUR CENTERS

1. Go to: **www.manhattanprep.com/gmat/studentcenter**
2. Log in with the username and password you chose when setting up your account.

IF YOU PURCHASED THIS BOOK AT A RETAIL LOCATION

1. Go to: **www.manhattanprep.com/gmat/access**
2. Create an account or, if you already have one, log in on this page with your username and password.
3. Follow the instructions on the screen.

Your one year of online access begins on the day that you register your book at the above URL.

You only need to register your product ONCE at the above URL. To use your online resources any time AFTER you have completed the registration process, log in to the following URL:
www.manhattanprep.com/gmat/studentcenter

Please note that online access is nontransferable. This means that only NEW and UNREGISTERED copies of the book will grant you online access. Previously used books will NOT provide any online resources.

IF YOU PURCHASED AN EBOOK VERSION OF THIS BOOK

1. Create an account with Manhattan Prep at this website:
www.manhattanprep.com/gmat/register
2. Email a copy of your purchase receipt to **gmat@manhattanprep.com** to activate your resources. Please be sure to use the same email address to create an account that you used to purchase the eBook.

For any questions, email **gmat@manhattanprep.com** or call **800-576-4628**.

Please refer to the following page for a description of the online resources that come with this book.

YOUR ONLINE RESOURCES
YOUR PURCHASE INCLUDES ONLINE ACCESS TO THE FOLLOWING:

1 FULL-LENGTH GMAT PRACTICE EXAM

The full-length GMAT practice exam included with this book is delivered online using Manhattan Prep's proprietary computer-adaptive test engine. The exam adapts to your ability level by drawing from a bank of more than 500 unique questions of varying difficulty levels written by Manhattan Prep's expert instructors, all of whom have scored in the 99th percentile on the Official GMAT. At the end of the exam you will receive a score, an analysis of your results, and the opportunity to review detailed explanations for each question.

Important Note: The GMAT exam included with the purchase of this book is the same exam that you receive upon purchasing any book in the Manhattan Prep GMAT Complete Strategy Guide Set.

5 FREE INTERACT™ LESSONS

Interact™ is a comprehensive self-study program that is fun, intuitive, and directed by you. Each interactive video lesson is taught by an expert Manhattan Prep instructor and includes dozens of individual branching points. The choices you make determine the content you see. This book comes with access to the first five lessons of GMAT Interact. Lessons are available on your computer or iPad so you can prep where you are, when you want. For more information on the full version of this program, visit **manhattanprep.com/gmat/interact**.

CRITICAL REASONING ONLINE QUESTION BANK

The Online Question Bank for Critical Reasoning consists of 25 extra practice questions (with detailed explanations) that test the variety of concepts and skills covered in this book. These questions provide you with extra practice beyond the problem sets contained in this book. You may use our online timer to practice your pacing by setting time limits for each question in the bank.

ONLINE UPDATES TO THE CONTENT IN THIS BOOK

The content presented in this book is updated periodically to ensure that it reflects the GMAT's most current trends. You may view all updates, including any known errors or changes, upon registering for online access.

The above resources can be found in your Student Center at manhattanprep.com/gmat/studentcenter.

TABLE *of* CONTENTS

Official Guide Problem Sets   11

1. Argument Structure   13
  Problem Set   27

2. Methodology   33
  Problem Set   51

3. Structure-Based Family   57
  Problem Set   75

4. The Assumption Family: Find the Assumption   93
  Problem Set   107

5. The Assumption Family: Strengthen and Weaken   121
  Problem Set   145

6. The Assumption Family: Evaluate the Argument and Find the Flaw   173
  Problem Set   189

7. Evidence Family   205
  Problem Set   225

8. Wrong Answer Analysis   241
  Problem Set   251

guide **6**

Official Guide Problem Sets

As you work through this strategy guide, it is a very good idea to test your skills using official problems that appeared on the real GMAT in the past. To help you with this step of your studies, we have classified all of the problems from the three main *Official Guide* books and devised some problem sets to accompany this book.

These problem sets live in your Manhattan Prep Student Center so that they can be updated whenever the test makers update their books. When you log into your Student Center, click on the link for the *Official Guide Problem Sets*, found on your home page. Download them today!

The problem sets consist of three broad groups of questions:

1. A final quiz: Take this quiz after completing this entire guide.

2. A full practice set of questions: If you are taking one of our classes, this is the homework given on your syllabus, so just follow the syllabus assignments. If you are not taking one of our classes, you can do this practice set whenever you feel that you have a very solid understanding of the material taught in this guide.

3. A full reference list of all *Official Guide* problems that test the topics covered in this strategy guide: Use these problems to test yourself on specific topics or to create larger sets of mixed questions.

As you begin studying, try one problem at a time and review it thoroughly before moving on. In the middle of your studies, attempt some mixed sets of problems from a small pool of topics (the two quizzes we've devised for you are good examples of how to do this). Later in your studies, mix topics from multiple guides and include some questions that you've chosen randomly out of the *Official Guide*. This way, you'll learn to be prepared for anything!

Study Tips:

1. DO time yourself when answering questions.

2. DO cut yourself off and make a guess if a question is taking too long. You can try it again later without a time limit, but first practice the behavior you want to exhibit on the real test: let go and move on.

3. DON'T answer all of the *Official Guide* questions by topic or chapter at once. The real test will toss topics at you in random order, and half of the battle is figuring out what each new question is testing. Set yourself up to learn this when doing practice sets.

Chapter 1
of
Critical Reasoning

Argument Structure

In This Chapter...

The Core

Building Blocks of an Argument

Signal Words

Intermediate Conclusions and the Therefore Test

Chapter 1

Argument Structure

Here is an example of a typical GMAT argument in a Critical Reasoning (CR) problem:

> The expansion of the runways at the Bay City Airport will allow larger planes to use the airport. These new planes will create a large amount of noise, a nuisance for residents who live near the airport. However, many of the residents in this neighborhood work in construction, and the contract to expand the runways has been awarded to a local construction company. Thus, the expansion of the runways will lead to an increased quality of life for the residents of this neighborhood.

In order to solve CR problems effectively and efficiently, you need to pay close attention to the specific information given for that problem, while keeping in mind how to reason through a problem of that type.

For every question, you should begin by understanding what you are *given*:

> What is this author actually arguing?
> What are the pieces of this argument?
> How do they fit together?

Think about these questions in relation to the argument above before you keep reading.

On the GMAT:

1. All arguments contain at least one **premise**. A premise is information used by the author to support some claim or conclusion. That information may be a fact or an opinion. In the above example, sentence 3 is a premise because it helps to support the author's conclusion.

2. Most (though not all) arguments contain a **conclusion**, the primary claim the author is trying to prove or the outcome of a plan that someone is proposing. In the above example, sentence 4 is a conclusion.

3. Many arguments (though not all) contain **background** information, which provides context to allow you to understand the basic situation. The information is true but does not either support or go against the conclusion. In the above example, sentence 1 provides background.

4. Some arguments contain a **counterpoint** or **counterpremise**—a piece of information that goes against the author's conclusion. In the above example, sentence 2 represents a counterpoint because it goes against the author's conclusion.

Collectively, these categories represent the **building blocks** of an argument. How do you know which sentences fall into which categories? Try to articulate your own thought process for the argument above, then take a look at the decision process of this fictional student:

Argument	Reader's Thoughts
The expansion of the runways at the Bay City Airport will allow larger planes to use the airport.	*Hmm. This is a fact. It could be a **premise** or it could just be background. I'm not sure yet.*
These new planes will create a large amount of noise, a nuisance for residents who live near the airport.	*Now they're moving into claim territory. Something negative will come from this project. Why are they telling me this? I can't figure that out until I know the conclusion.*
However, many of the residents in this neighborhood work in construction, and the contract to expand the runways has been awarded to a local construction company.	*The word "however" indicates a contrast between sentences 2 and 3. What's the contrast? The noise is a negative consequence of the expansion, while winning a work contract is a positive consequence. Looks like I've got a **premise** and a **counterpoint** in these two sentences, but I don't know which one is which yet.*
Thus, the expansion of the runways will lead to an increased quality of life for the residents of this neighborhood.	*The word "thus" usually indicates a **conclusion**. Yes, this does seem like a conclusion—this project will have a certain outcome (better quality of life in this neighborhood), and I can now see how the previous two sentences fit into this conclusion. Sentence 3 is a **premise** because it provides one way in which the quality of life might be better for these people (they might make more money), and sentence 2 is a **counterpremise** because it tells me a negative consequence.*

Notice how many times the reader thought, "I'm not sure yet" (or something along those lines). That will happen frequently while reading an argument. You're gathering information and trying to understand what each piece might be, but you won't really know how everything fits together until you know what the conclusion is—and that might not be until the end of the argument. Here's the argument again, with each sentence labeled:

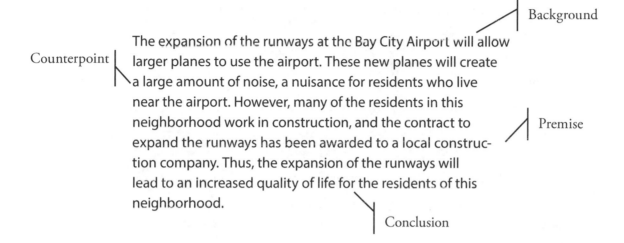

The Core

The premise (or premises) and conclusion represent the **core** of the argument. Remember that not all arguments will have a conclusion, but all will have at least one premise, so you will always have at least a partial core. The core represents what the author is trying to tell you or prove to you.

In this problem, the core consists of these two pieces:

However, many of the residents in this neighborhood work in construction, and the contract to expand the runways has been awarded to a local construction company.

Thus, the expansion of the runways will lead to an increased quality of life for the residents of this neighborhood.

Premise: provides one piece of evidence toward the conclusion

Conclusion: the claim supported by the given evidence

The argument is not airtight. For example, do you know for sure that residents of the neighborhood work for the local construction company that won the contract? If they don't, then perhaps residents won't benefit after all. As you'll see later in this book, that kind of reasoning will help when you get to the question-answering stage.

Building Blocks of an Argument

Here are the **building blocks** discussed so far:

Premise

- Is part of the **core** of the argument; present in every argument.

- Supports the author's conclusion.

- Can be a fact or an opinion; can be a description, historical information, data, or a comparison of things.

- Is often signaled by words or phrases such as *because of, since, due to,* or *as a result of.*

Conclusion

- Is part of the **core** of an argument; present in most arguments.

- Represents the author's main opinion or claim; can be in the form of a prediction, a judgment of quality or merit, a statement of causality, or the outcome of a plan.

- Is supported by at least one **premise.**

- Is often signaled by words such as *therefore, thus, so,* or *consequently* (although harder arguments might use such a word elsewhere in the argument in an attempt to confuse you).

Background

- Is not part of the **core**; not always present.

- Provides context to help understand the **core**; similar to premises but less important to the argument itself.

- Is almost always fact-based; can be in almost any form: historical information, data, descriptions of plans or ideas, definitions of words or concepts, and so on.

Counterpoint or Counterpremise

- Is not part of the **core**; only present occasionally.

- Opposes or goes against the author's **conclusion** in some way.

- Introduces multiple opportunities for traps: believing that the **conclusion** is the opposite of what it is, mistakenly thinking that a **counterpoint** is a **premise** (and vice versa), and so on.

- Is often signaled by a transition word such as *although, though, however, yet,* and *but* (recognize, though, that the counterpoint may come before such words).

Argument Structure

The argument above used all four of the building blocks in this order:

Background – Counterpoint – Premise – Conclusion

MANHATTAN
PREP

The simplest possible argument will contain only premises. Its structure might look like this:

Premise – Premise

The GMAT can vary the types of building blocks used in a particular argument, and it can also vary the order of those building blocks. If you can categorize the building blocks given in any particular argument, you're one step closer to answering the question correctly.

Next are some sample arguments. You have two tasks. First, read the argument and try to identify the role of each sentence or major piece of information (note that one sentence could contain two different pieces of information). Use that information to jot down the premise(s) and conclusion. Second, try to articulate in your own words *how* the premise(s) support the conclusion.

1. Budget Fitness will grow its membership base by 10% in the next six months. Budget Fitness has recently crafted a clever ad campaign that it plans to air on several local radio stations.

2. Last year, the Hudson Family Farm was not profitable. However, the farm will be profitable this year. The farm operators have planted cotton, rather than corn, in several fields. Because cotton prices are expected to rise dramatically this year, the farm can expect larger revenues from cotton sales than it previously earned from corn.

Answers can be found on page 25.

Signal Words

Certain words can provide valuable clues as to whether you've got a conclusion, a premise, or a counterpoint. If an argument says "Adnan will earn a high test score because he has studied hard," the word *because* signals a cause–effect relationship. One thing (he has studied hard) is supposed to lead to another (he will earn a high score on the test). The premise here is the cause that follows the *because*, and the conclusion is the claimed result.

Finish the following exchange:

Sam: Can I borrow your car?

Marie: Even though you don't have a driver's license …

What is Marie likely to say next? She has acknowledged a reason that she should *not* let Sam borrow her car, but her sentence implies that she's about to let him borrow it anyway. (Not very wise, Marie!)

What if the conversation had gone this way?

Sam: Can I borrow your car?

Marie: I like you, Sam. However, you don't have a driver's license, so …

This time, Marie's not falling for Sam's charming smile! She's about to deny him access to her car.

What's the difference? How do you know that, in the first case, Marie seems willing to lend Sam her car while, in the second case, she isn't going to do so?

Signal words! The term *even though* signals an acknowledgment of or a concession to an opposing point of view. Even though it's true that Sam doesn't have a driver's license, Marie will still let him borrow her car. The contrast word *however*, on the other hand, flips a switch: Marie may like Sam, BUT she's not about to let him use her car when he doesn't even have a driver's license.

You can use these kinds of language clues to help you classify information in arguments.

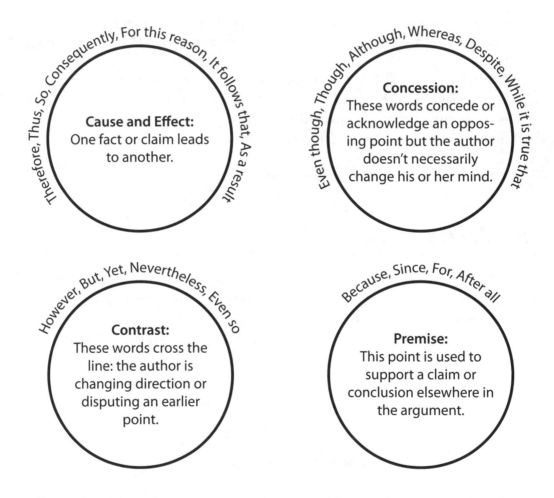

You likely know most or all of these words already, but you might not have consciously considered why they're used in certain contexts. Start paying attention! These signal words will make your job easier during the test.

Intermediate Conclusions and the Therefore Test

You have one more building block to learn in this chapter. Read and deconstruct the argument below:

> The owner of a small publishing company plans to lease a new office space that has floor-to-ceiling windows and no internal walls, arguing that the new space will enhance worker productivity. The owner cites a recent study showing that workers exposed to natural light throughout the day tended to report, on average, a higher level of job satisfaction than did those who worked in office spaces that used fluorescent lighting. Thus, the owner concluded, exposure to natural light has a positive effect on workers' job satisfaction.

The owner of a small publishing company plans to lease a new office space that has floor-to-ceiling windows and no internal walls,	*This is likely to be background information because it introduces a plan to do something but no actual claim (yet). The argument is probably about the plan, or a result of the plan.*
arguing that the new space will enhance worker productivity.	*This might be the conclusion because it describes the predicted future benefit of the company's plan.*
The owner cites a recent study showing that workers exposed to natural light throughout the day tended to report, on average, a higher level of job satisfaction than did those who worked in office spaces that used fluorescent lighting.	*This seems to be a premise in support of that conclusion. The workers will be more productive because the new space will provide exposure to natural light through the floor-to-ceiling windows.*
Thus, the owner concluded, exposure to natural light has a positive effect on workers' job satisfaction.	*Hmm, this is strange. This appears to be the conclusion as well. It uses the word "thus," it represents an explanation for the study's results, and it even says that "the owner concluded" this!*

This is a tough one! In this case, you have *two* claims that could be conclusions. Now what?

This brings you to another building block, the **intermediate conclusion** (also known as the secondary conclusion). What is an intermediate conclusion? Look at this simpler example:

> The burglar is clumsy and often makes a lot of noise while robbing homes. As a result, he is more likely to get caught. Thus, in the near future, he will probably end up in jail.

The first sentence is a basic premise: it indicates some factual information about the robber. The second sentence is a claim made based upon that premise: *because* he makes noise, he is more likely to get caught. This is a conclusion...but, wait, there's a third sentence! That third sentence also contains a claim, and this claim follows from the previous claim: *because* he is more likely to get caught, there is a good chance he will end up in jail.

1

Essentially, a premise supports a conclusion, and that conclusion then supports a further conclusion. If you place the events in logical order, then the first conclusion can be called the **intermediate conclusion**. The second conclusion can be called the final conclusion to distinguish it from the intermediate conclusion. Alternatively, you might reserve the word conclusion for the final conclusion, and call the intermediate conclusion another premise—just recognize that it's a claim that is supported by other premises and that in turn supports the (final) conclusion.

Either way, how do you figure out which is which? Use the Therefore Test. Call the two claims *A* (he's more likely to get caught) and *B* (he will probably end up in jail). Plug the two claims into two sentences using *Because* and *Therefore* and ask yourself which one is true:

> BECAUSE *A* (he's more likely to get caught), THEREFORE *B* (he will probably end up in jail).
>
> OR
>
> BECAUSE *B* (he will probably end up in jail), THEREFORE *A* (he's more likely to get caught).

(Using both *Because* and *Therefore* may seem like overkill, but it ensures that you keep the roles straight!) Which sentence makes more sense to you? The first scenario makes sense, but the second one doesn't. The fact that he will probably end up in jail should follow the *Therefore*, so it is the final, real conclusion. The fact that he's more likely to get caught follows the *Because*, so it is only an intermediate conclusion.

In the burglar passage above, the three pieces were presented in logical progression: **Premise – Intermediate Conclusion – Final Conclusion**. Arguments won't always follow this logical order, however; they might mix up the order and toss in additional information.

Try the Therefore Test with the job satisfaction argument. You have two possible conclusions:

1. (*A*) … arguing that the new space will enhance worker productivity.
2. (*B*) Thus, the owner concluded, exposure to natural light has a positive effect on workers' job satisfaction.

Which scenario makes more sense?

> BECAUSE the new space will enhance worker productivity,
> THEREFORE exposure to natural light has a positive effect on workers' job satisfaction.
>
> OR
>
> BECAUSE exposure to natural light has a positive effect on workers' job satisfaction,
> THEREFORE the new space will enhance worker productivity.

The second scenario makes more sense, so (*B*) is the intermediate conclusion and (*A*) is the final conclusion.

As is typical of arguments with an intermediate conclusion, the premise supports the intermediate conclusion, which then supports the final conclusion:

A study found a correlation between natural lighting and job satisfaction.

The owner concludes that exposure to natural light causes better job satisfaction.

The owner then concludes that the new, light-filled space will enhance productivity.

Here's the original argument again:

> The owner of a small publishing company plans to lease a new office space that has floor-to-ceiling windows and no internal walls, arguing that the new space will enhance worker productivity. The owner cites a recent study showing that workers exposed to natural light throughout the day tended to report, on average, a higher level of job satisfaction than did those who worked in office spaces that used fluorescent lighting. Thus, the owner concluded, exposure to natural light has a positive effect on workers' job satisfaction.

The argument begins with **background** information, then goes straight into the final **conclusion**. Next, you're given a **premise** followed by an **intermediate conclusion**.

As the argument above demonstrates, the logical structure of a GMAT argument can get a little complicated. If there is more than one logical step, make sure that your understanding is firm before you attempt to answer the question.

1

Cheat Sheet

Argument Structure Cheat Sheet

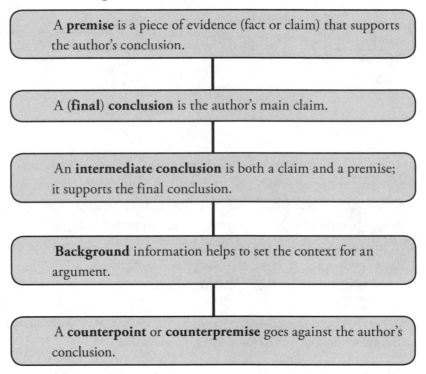

A **premise** is a piece of evidence (fact or claim) that supports the author's conclusion.

A (**final**) **conclusion** is the author's main claim.

An **intermediate conclusion** is both a claim and a premise; it supports the final conclusion.

Background information helps to set the context for an argument.

A **counterpoint** or **counterpremise** goes against the author's conclusion.

These building blocks will help you to understand the structure of an argument and answer the question.

When there is more than one conclusion or claim, use the **Therefore Test** to find the final conclusion. One of these two scenarios will work: either "BECAUSE A is true, THEREFORE B is true" or "BECAUSE B is true, THEREFORE A is true" The claim that follows the *Therefore* in the working scenario is the final, real conclusion.

Answer Key

1.

Budget Fitness will grow its membership base by 10% in the next six months.	*This is a prediction about the future, so it is a claim, not a fact. This is a good candidate to be the conclusion.*
Budget Fitness has recently crafted a clever ad campaign that it plans to air on several local radio stations.	*Budget Fitness already crafted the campaign— this is a fact. It is also a fact that the company currently "plans" to air the campaign (though whether it will actually air is uncertain, since that is a future event). This information supports the claim in the first sentence, so it is a premise.*

(Task 1) The order of the parts is **Conclusion – Premise**. If you rewrite it as Premise → Conclusion, then you have something such as this:

> BF has ad to air on radio → BF will grow members 10% in 6 mos

(Task 2) The author claims that the gym *will* increase its membership in the future *because* the company will launch an ad campaign. Presumably, the company thinks that this campaign will help attract new customers.

2.

Last year, the Hudson Family Farm was not profitable.	*This is a fact; it already occurred in the past. This may be background info, a premise, or a counterpoint.*
However, the farm will be profitable this year.	*The word "however" indicates a change in direction. This prediction is the <u>opposite</u> of what happened last year. This future prediction is a good candidate to be the conclusion, in which case the previous sentence would be a counterpoint.*
The farm operators have planted cotton, rather than corn, in several fields.	*This is a fact. Hmm, why does it matter which crop the farm is planting?*
Because cotton prices are expected to rise dramatically this year, the farm can expect larger revenues from cotton sales than it previously earned from corn.	*Okay, planting cotton will lead to more revenue than was earned last year. The author is using this information to support his conclusion in sentence two.*

1

(Task 1) The order of the parts is **Counterpoint – Conclusion – Premise – Premise**. Reordering as Premises → Conclusion, you get this:

> Cotton prices will be higher and the farm is planting cotton → The farm will be profitable this year

(Task 2) The argument predicts that an unprofitable farm *will* become profitable *because* a change in crops will result in higher revenues.

Did you spot any flaws in the author's reasoning? There are several, but the biggest one is the fact that revenues and profits are not the same thing! A company can have lots of revenue and zero profit—or even lose money.

MANHATTAN
PREP

Problem Set

Identify the role of each sentence or major piece of information. Use that information to write out the building block structure.

1. A program instituted by a state government to raise money allows homeowners to prepay their future property taxes at the current rate. Even if the government were to raise the tax rate in a subsequent year, any prepaid taxes would allow the homeowner to maintain taxes at the lower rate, lowering the overall property tax burden over time. For this reason, homeowners should participate in the program.

2. Tay-Sachs disease, a usually fatal genetic condition caused by the buildup of gangliocides in nerve cells, occurs more frequently among Ashkenazi Jews than among the general population. The age of onset is typically six months and generally results in death by the age of four.

3. Some critics have argued that the price of food and drink at Ultralux, a restaurant, is too high for the quality offered. However, Ultralux features a beautiful interior and comfortable seating, and research has shown that consumers actually enjoy food and drink more in such a setting, even when the food and drink are of comparable quality to the food and drink served elsewhere. Thus, the food and drink at Ultralux are reasonably priced.

4. Editorial: To stem the influx of illegal immigrants, the government is planning to construct a wall along our entire border with Country Y. This wall, however, will do little to actually reduce the number of illegal immigrants. Because few economic opportunities exist in Country Y, individuals will simply develop other creative ways to enter our nation.

5. The cutback in physical education is the primary contributing factor to North High School's increasing failure rate on the year-end physical fitness examination. Last year, when students participated in gym class on a daily basis, 85% of the school's seniors passed the exam. This year, students had gym class twice weekly, and only 70% of seniors passed the test. Clearly, fewer sessions of gym class lead to reduced fitness.

Solutions

1.

A program instituted by a state government to raise money allows homeowners to prepay their future property taxes at the current rate.	*This is a fact. It sounds like background, though it could be a premise—not sure yet. People can choose to pay future taxes right now at the current tax rate. Someone would only want to do this if it saved money.*
Even if the government were to raise the tax rate in a subsequent year, any prepaid taxes would allow the homeowner to maintain taxes at the lower rate, lowering the overall property tax burden over time.	*Ah, here's how it could save money. This is a premise. If taxes go up but you've already pre-paid, you don't have to pay more; you get to pay at the lower rate. What if tax rates go down? What if you sell your house?*
For this reason, homeowners should participate in the program.	*Conclusion: people should participate. But what if it doesn't save them money? Seems like the conclusion should be: if this will save someone money, then that person should participate.*

The structure is **Background – Premise – Conclusion**. The author concludes that people should participate *because* they would save money *if* taxes go up.

2.

Tay-Sachs disease, a usually fatal genetic condition caused by the buildup of gangliocides in nerve cells, occurs more frequently among Ashkenazi Jews than among the general population.	*This is a fact. It could be background info or a premise.*
The age of onset is typically six months and generally results in death by the age of four.	*This is also a fact— just more information about this disease. That's interesting. There's no conclusion here, just two facts. Both are premises.*

The structure is **Premise – Premise**. The argument concludes nothing. (Note: two types of questions lack conclusions: Inference and Explain a Discrepancy. You'll learn about these later in the book.)

1

3.

Some critics have argued that the price of food and drink at Ultralux, a restaurant, is too high for the quality offered.	*"Some critics" criticize the restaurant Ultralux for being too expensive. The language "**some** critics" is often used in counterpoints; later, the author will often say something else that the author or others believe instead.*
However, Ultralux features a beautiful interior and comfortable seating,	*This seems to be pointing out a good thing about Ultralux.*
and research has shown that consumers actually enjoy food and drink more in such a setting, even when the food and drink are of comparable quality to the food and drink served elsewhere.	*This indicates why the beautiful interior and comfortable seating are beneficial. If you enjoy the food and drink more, then perhaps you're willing to pay more money?*
Thus, the food and drink at Ultralux are reasonably priced.	*This looks like a conclusion. In fact, it directly contradicts the critics' argument in the first sentence, which you can now be sure is a counterpoint.*

The structure is **Counterpoint – Premise – Premise – Conclusion**. The author concludes that Ultralux is reasonably priced *because* research demonstrates that certain beneficial aspects provided by the restaurant are valuable to the consumer.

4.

Editorial: To stem the influx of illegal immigrants, the government is planning to construct a wall along our entire border with Country Y.	*The government plans to construct a wall and claims that this will reduce the number of illegal immigrants. This could be the conclusion, but the sentence also starts with the word "Editorial," implying that someone other than the government is writing this argument. Read on to see whether that person gives a different opinion or claim.*
This wall, however, will do little to actually reduce the number of illegal immigrants.	*"However!" Okay, whoever's writing the editorial thinks that the government's plan is not going to achieve its objective. This goes against the previous sentence and represents the author's point of view, so the previous sentence must be a counterpremise.*
Because few economic opportunities exist in Country Y, individuals will simply develop other creative ways to enter our nation.	*"Because"—here's the reason why the Editorial writer thinks this: the people in Country Y have no real opportunities in their own country, so they will just search for other ways to get into the neighboring country.*

MANHATTAN
PREP

The structure is **Counterpoint – Conclusion – Premise**. The author concludes that the government's plan won't work *because* the people trying to immigrate illegally will just search for other ways to do so, since they still won't have many opportunities in their home country.

5.

The cutback in physical education is the primary contributing factor to North High School's increasing failure rate on the year-end physical fitness examination.	*This is an opinion, so it could be the conclusion. The school isn't offering as much physical education as it used to, and the author claims that this is causing more students to fail a physical fitness exam.*
Last year, when students participated in gym class on a daily basis, 85% of the school's seniors passed the exam.	*Fact. Last year, they had gym class daily, and the vast majority of students passed the exam.*
This year, students had gym class twice weekly, and only 70% of seniors passed the test.	*Fact. This year, they had gym class less frequently, and a smaller percentage of students passed the exam.*
Clearly, fewer sessions of gym class lead to reduced fitness.	*Here's another claim. Having fewer gym classes causes reduced fitness levels. Is this the conclusion? What about the first sentence?*

Try the Therefore Test: A = cutback in gym is causing more kids to fail the fitness exam; B = cutback in gym causes reduced fitness.

> *BECAUSE cutbacks in gym are causing kids to fail the exam, THEREFORE those cutbacks are causing reduced fitness?*

> *BECAUSE cutbacks in gym are causing reduced fitness, THEREFORE those cutbacks are causing more kids to fail the fitness exam?*

It's the second option—first, the kids experience reduced fitness, and then that causes them to fail the fitness exam. The first sentence is the final conclusion, and the last sentence is just an intermediate conclusion.

The structure is **Final Conclusion – Premise – Premise – Intermediate Conclusion**. The author concludes that gym cutbacks are causing kids to fail the fitness exam *because* this year's seniors had fewer gym classes, leading to reduced fitness levels that, in turn, caused more kids to fail the exam.

Chapter 2

of

Critical Reasoning

Methodology

In This Chapter...

Step 1: Identify the Question

Step 2: Deconstruct the Argument

Step 3: State the Goal

Step 4: Work from Wrong to Right

How to Map an Argument

Chapter 2
Methodology

In Chapter 1, you learned about argument building blocks and examined how to "deconstruct" an argument in order to understand how the pieces of information are related. These tasks represent the first two steps of the overall four-step approach for any Critical Reasoning problem.

Before diving into the four-step process, let's discuss what you *don't* want to do. While you have a lot of flexibility in how you work your way through the problem, there are some approaches that are downright bad, such as this one:

1. Read the argument pretty quickly, don't write anything down, don't understand the "big picture."

2. Read the question.

3. Realize you need to read the argument again in order to answer; re-read the argument.

4. Re-read the question.

5. Examine the answers, eliminating one or several.

6. Read the argument for the third time.

7. Eliminate another answer.

8. Start checking each remaining answer against the argument and re-reading the argument.

9. Repeat until one answer is left.

What's the problem? That's incredibly inefficient! If you've ever taken any standardized test before, you know that these tests have serious time pressure. The GMAT is no exception. In fact, you need to average about two minutes per CR question. So what do you do instead?

2

Use Manhattan Prep's four-step approach for all CR questions:

Step 1: Identify the question.

Step 2: Deconstruct the argument.

Step 3: State the goal.

Step 4: Work from wrong to right.

Step 1: Identify the Question

Most arguments are followed by a question (you'll learn about one exception later). The wording of the question stem allows you to identify which type of question you're about to answer. You will need to employ different kinds of reasoning for different types of questions, so you want to know, right from the start, what kind of question you have.

There are three broad categories of Critical Reasoning questions: the Structure-based family, the Assumption-based family, and the Evidence-based family. Each of these families contains a few distinct question types. In later chapters, you'll learn how to identify all of the question types.

The Structure-Based Family

These questions ask you to determine something based upon the building blocks of the argument. What pieces are included in the argument and how do they fit together? The two types of Structure questions will be discussed in Chapter 3:

Question Type	Sample Question Phrasing	Goal
Describe the Role	In the argument given, the two boldface portions play which of the following roles?	Identify the roles (building blocks) of the boldface portions of the argument.
Describe the Argument	In the passage, the mayor challenges the councilmember's argument by doing which of the following?	Describe how a certain piece of information affects the argument.

MANHATTAN
PREP

2

The Assumption-Based Family

These questions all depend upon an understanding of the **assumptions** made by the author to reach a certain conclusion. What is an assumption?

First, an assumption is something that the author *does not state* in the argument; for this reason, such assumptions are called *unstated*. An assumption is, however, something that the author *must believe to be true* in order to draw the given conclusion. Without the assumption, the argument fails.

You'll learn much more about assumptions in Chapter 4; take a look at this short example:

> That car is green. Therefore, that car cannot belong to Dan.

If you're told only that the car is green, how can you know for sure that it doesn't belong to Dan? Clearly, there's some information missing. What is the author assuming here?

> Assumption: Dan does not have a green car.

If you were to insert the assumption into the argument, it would make the argument better:

> That car is green. Dan does not have a green car. Therefore, that car cannot belong to Dan.

In this case, it not only makes the argument better, it makes the argument "airtight"—nobody can argue with the conclusion now! That usually won't happen on the GMAT, but an assumption should plug a hole in the argument. The assumption will be necessary to the argument; that is, if the assumption *isn't* true, the argument breaks down.

There are five types of Assumption questions, which will be covered in Chapters 4, 5, and 6 as shown below:

Question Type	Sample Question Phrasing	Goal
Find the Assumption	The argument depends on which of the following assumptions?	Identify an unstated assumption.
Strengthen the Argument	Which of the following, if true, provides the most support for the argument above?	Identify a new piece of information that strengthens the author's argument.
Weaken the Argument	Which of the following, if true, most seriously weakens the argument?	Identify a new piece of information that weakens the author's argument.

| Evaluate the Argument | Which of the following must be studied in order to evaluate the argument above? | Identify a piece of information that would help to determine the soundness of the argument. |
| Find the Flaw | Which of the following indicates a flaw in the reasoning above? | Identify something illogical in the argument. |

The Evidence-Based Family

These arguments all lack conclusions; they consist entirely of premises! They also won't include any assumptions. You're asked to find something that *must be true* or something that *eliminates a discrepancy* in order to answer the question. You'll learn more about both of these question types in Chapter 7.

Question Type	Sample Question Phrasing	Goal
Inference	Which of the following can be logically concluded from the passage above?	Identify something that must be true based on the given information.
Explain a Discrepancy	Which of the following, if true, most helps to explain the surprising finding?	Identify a new piece of information that eliminates some apparent paradox in the argument.

This book also discusses a variation called Complete the Argument in a separate chapter. This variation is not a different question type; rather, it's a different way of presenting one of the other question types.

As you go through each of the families and their question types, you will learn what kind of language signals specific question types—and that's your first big step in the four-step approach: Identify the Question.

Step 2: Deconstruct the Argument

Now that you've identified the family and question type, you can use that information to deconstruct the argument. You began to learn how to do this in Chapter 1 when you labeled arguments using the building block components.

At this stage, many people take a few light notes. If Critical Reasoning is already a strength for you and you don't write anything, then you may not need to start. If, on the other hand, you want to improve CR significantly, then making an Argument Map will likely be one of your necessary strategies.

Revisit the first argument from Chapter 1. As you deconstruct the argument, jot down an abbreviated "map" of the argument.

> The expansion of the runways at the Bay City Airport will allow larger planes to use the airport. These new planes will create a large amount of noise, a nuisance for residents who live near the airport. However, many of the residents in this neighborhood work in construction, and the contract to expand the runways has been awarded to a local construction company. Thus, the expansion of the runways will lead to an increased quality of life for the residents of this neighborhood.

Here's one method of notetaking, idea by idea:

> BC ↑ rnwy → ↑ P →> noise
>
> BUT res work in constr [so work for them?]
>
> ⓒ plan → better life for res

This map may seem cryptic by itself, but remember, you will always have access to the argument on your screen. You do not have to answer the question using only your notes. In fact, if you are taking too many notes, it can be helpful to imagine that you cannot use those notes to answer the question. The process of creating them is what matters.

You should avoid writing down full sentences. You should try to abbreviate dramatically, even reducing whole words to single letters on the fly, as was done above:

> BC = Bay City Airport
>
> ↑ = expansion, larger
>
> rnwy = runway
>
> → = therefore
>
> P = planes
>
> res = residents
>
> constr = construction

If these abbreviations are too cryptic for you, of course, make them longer. But if you practice, you'll be amazed by how much you can abbreviate. Some of your abbreviations will be one-off creations; others you'll use all the time (e.g., a right arrow to mean *therefore*). The goal as you create these notes is not to re-create every detail of the argument, but rather to help your brain understand the argument in real time. An effective map will summarize the core of the argument, including the premises and the conclusion. Now that you've delineated the parts of the argument for yourself, you'll be in a better position to answer the question.

Here are a few tips for effective notetaking on the fly. First, most people would probably write down only the info from the first sentence first:

BC ↑ rnwy → ↑ P

Then, as you continue reading, you might realize that the second sentence follows from the first: those bigger planes then cause more noise. As a result, you might choose to continue writing on the same line, even though the additional information is given in a separate sentence. In this fashion, you are linking together the parts of the argument.

Second, did you note the question in the brackets: [so work for them?] Why is that there? The argument says that many residents work in construction. It also says a local company was awarded the contract to do the work. Did you notice anything missing? The argument never actually said that the residents of this neighborhood work for the local construction company. That might be something to think about as you try to answer the question. Feel free to jot down any thoughts you have about the argument, in particular its holes, as you go. Just be sure to bracket those thoughts, so that you don't ever think they're part of the argument itself.

Not everyone writes this much; some people don't write anything at all. Practice to determine what works best for you. At first, you might write down too much and get bogged down. Keep practicing for at least a few weeks; as you gain skill, you'll discover how fast you can take useful, highly abbreviated notes.

Step 3: State the Goal

This is a short but crucial step: what exactly are you trying to do when you answer this question? What's your goal? At this stage, you know what kind of question you have, you (hopefully) understand the argument and how it fits together, and you know the conclusion (if there is one). What's next?

Remind yourself of your goal, which depends upon the type of question given. Each question type requires a certain kind of reasoning and demands certain characteristics from the correct answer. For instance, imagine that the question for the Bay City Airport argument asks you to Find the Assumption. In that case, your goal is to find something that the author must believe to be true in claiming that the expansion of the runways will lead to an increased quality of life for neighborhood residents.

You'll learn the goals for each question type as you work through this guide.

Step 4: Work from Wrong to Right

Finally, the answer choices! On GMAT Verbal in general, you're asked to find the "best" answer. You're going to use a two-step process to do so:

1. First, look through all five answers and eliminate as many "definitely wrong" answers as you can. Do *not* try to decide which is the *right* answer right now. Instead, concentrate on eliminating *wrong* answers.

2. If you have only one answer left after this first pass, great; you're done. If you have two or more answers left, then compare those remaining answers.

Why do you want to attack the answers this way, "working from wrong to right?" By definition, finding the *best* answer is a comparison; if you spot a tempting wrong answer, you might not be able to spot what is wrong with it until you've read the right answer. It's most efficient to dump all of the "No way!" answers as fast as you can, and then directly compare the remaining, more tempting answers. Of course, there will always be only one right answer, but your final choice will be made easier if you have already eliminated the bad wrong answers.

Finally, remember one last tip for Verbal questions: when you've narrowed to two answers, compare those two answers just once more. Then pick and move on. Going back and forth multiple times is a waste of time—either you know it after comparing the first time, or you don't.

When you work from wrong to right, it's critical to keep track of your thinking on your scrap paper. You need to decide how to write down ABCDE and how to notate your thoughts.

Decision #1: How do I write down ABCDE?

Option 1	Pros	Cons
Write ABCDE for each question.	Can write on/cross off each letter; can keep letters right next to map about argument.	Have to write 41 separate times as you proceed through the Verbal section.

This option might look like this, if the first question is "Weaken the Argument" (noted with a "W") and the second question is "Strengthen the Argument" (noted with an "S"):

```
W  A B C D E

notes
notes

S  A B C D E

notes
notes
```

Option 2	Pros	Cons
Write ABCDE at the top of the page, then move to a new line for each question .	Only have to write once for each page (several times for entire test).	Have to keep track "below" each letter; map might not be right next to answer tracking row.

This option might look like the diagram below, in which the first question is Weaken and the second question is Strengthen. The scrap pad you'll be given is graph paper, so there will already be lincs built in to separate the five answer choices.

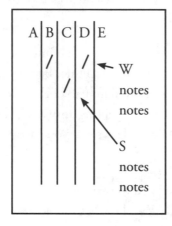

Decision #2: What symbols will I use to keep track of my thoughts?

You need four symbols. You can use any symbols you prefer as long as you consistently use the same symbols:

✗ or /	Definitely wrong
~	Maybe
?	I have no idea.
○	This is it!

MANHATTAN
PREP

Try these methods on an actual problem:

> Over the past decade, many companies have begun using automated telephone services: callers hear a machine-generated voice and are able to select options using the numbers on the telephone keypad. Research shows that callers are more patient when the machine-generated voice is that of a woman. Thus, smaller companies that cannot afford an automated service should consider hiring women, rather than men, to interact with customers by phone.
>
> Which of the following, if true, would be most damaging to the conclusion above?
>
> (A) Automated telephone services are becoming cheaper and cheaper every year.
> (B) Patient customers tend to order more products and return fewer products than impatient customers.
> (C) A separate study indicated that the extra patience exhibited by callers is limited to interactions with an automated system.
> (D) Some customers prefer automated systems to talking with a live person.
> (E) On average, callers are only slightly more patient when interacting with a female voice, rather than a male voice, in an automated telephone system.

How did you do with each step? Did you identify the question type? Do you feel comfortable with your map, and did you identify the conclusion (if there is one)? Did you remember to state the goal (briefly) before looking at the answers? Did you use the two-step process to assess the answer choices, working from wrong to right?

Here's how someone might work through the above problem, step by step. The table displays text from the problem, the student's thoughts, and the relevant notes on scrap paper.

Step 1: Identify the question.

Argument	Thoughts	Paper
Which of the following, if true, would be most damaging to the conclusion above?	*"Most damaging to the conclusion" means this is a Weaken. I need to find the conclusion, and I need to think about what flaws or gaps might exist in the argument.*	W A B C D E

Step 2: Deconstruct the argument.

Argument	Thoughts	Paper
Over the past decade, many companies have begun using automated telephone services;	*Sounds like background, but I'll jot down a note anyway.*	10y: co's use auto phone
callers hear a machine-generated voice and are able to select options using the numbers on the telephone keypad.	*This is describing what an automated phone system is; I probably don't need to write that down.*	
Research shows that callers are more patient when the machine-generated voice is that of a woman.	*This is a fact, not a claim, so it has to be either a premise or counter-premise. It's probably a premise, since there's only one sentence left.*	Res: female = ↑ patience
Thus, smaller companies that cannot afford an automated service should consider hiring women, rather than men, to interact with customers by phone.	*This is the only claim, so it's the conclusion. Now I can go back and add a © to the conclusion in my map and a + to the premise.*	Small co's → use women phone

The final map might look something like this:

W   A B C D E

10y: co's use auto phone

+ Res: female = ↑ patience

© Small co's → use women phone

Your map might look very different from the map above. That's perfectly fine as long as your map conveys to you the basic flow of information clearly and concisely as you put it together. Remember, the map is most useful as you make it, not as you look at it later.

Step 3: State the goal.

The question is a Weaken question, so briefly restate the main reasoning and conclusion of the argument. Remind yourself of your goal on the problem:

Small companies should hire women to answer the phones, because callers are more patient when hearing automated female voices.

I need to weaken that conclusion, so there's some reason why companies might not be better off hiring women to answer the phones.

Hmm. The evidence is about automated female voices, while the conclusion is about real women. Is there any kind of disconnect there?

MANHATTAN
PREP

<u>Step 4: Work from wrong to right.</u>

Now, attack the answers!

Argument	Thoughts	Paper
(A) Automated telephone services are becoming cheaper and cheaper every year.	*The conclusion discusses what companies should do when they <u>can't</u> afford automated services. This choice addresses those who can buy the service, so it's irrelevant to the argument.*	~~A~~
(B) Patient customers tend to order more products and return fewer products than impatient customers.	*This is a good reason for the company to do whatever it can to keep its customers in a patient mood. If anything, that would strengthen the argument.*	~~B~~
(C) A separate study indicated that the extra patience exhibited by callers is limited to interactions with an automated system.	*Hmm. This highlights a distinction between automated and live voices...I was wondering earlier whether that might be the disconnect. There doesn't seem to be any evidence now that a live female voice will make callers more patient. Keep this one in.*	<u>C</u>
(D) Some customers prefer automated systems to talking with a live person.	*This argument is about only those companies that <u>can't</u> afford the system and are using real people. Nope, this isn't it.*	~~D~~
(E) On average, callers are only slightly more patient when interacting with a female voice, rather than a male voice, in an automated telephone system.	*This one seems to be telling me there isn't a huge difference between male and female voices—but there is still a small positive effect for female voices. If anything, this strengthens the argument; after all, as a small business owner, I'll take any necessary steps that will get me more business! I've crossed off four answers, so (C) is the correct answer.*	~~E~~

At the end, the answer choice letters on your paper would look like this:

~~A~~   ~~B~~   Ⓒ   ~~D~~   ~~E~~

How to Map an Argument

A clear, consistent shorthand (abbreviation) method will help you to map the argument efficiently and spend more of your mental energy focused on how the argument works, rather than on how to write down a particular piece of information.

Initially, you may write too much (and take too long). Look over your map when reviewing practice problems: where could you have abbreviated even more heavily? Eventually, you will be able to abbreviate many things down to single letters or just one word and still remember what those abbreviations mean for the 60 to 90 seconds remaining until you finish the problem.

2

In fact, once you become an expert at this, your map should be abbreviated enough that, if you were to re-read it in a few days (after forgetting the argument), you would *not* be able to tell what the full argument was. If, a week later, you can reconstruct the entire argument just from your map, then you wrote down too much.

The chart below contains some symbols and abbreviations that you might find useful for Critical Reasoning. As you study, make sure to develop your own.

Increase/more/high	↑	Decrease/less/low	↓
Causes/leads to/results in	→	Was caused by	←
Greater than/more than/majority	>	Less than/smaller than/ minority	<
Equals/correlates with	=	Number	#
Price/dollar amount	$	Percent	%
Change	Δ	Women/Men	W/M
Best/most effective	H	Worst/least effective	×
Attribution (e.g., the Mayor said …)	: e.g. M:	Like/dislike	☺/☹
Future/prediction (something will happen, someone plans to do something)	F	Century (e.g., 20th century)	c e.g. 20c
Time	t	However/although/etc.	BUT
Years	y	Conclusion	Ⓒ
Your own thoughts (not in the argument)	[your own thoughts in brackets]	Profit, Revenue, Cost	P = R − C
Premise	+ (plus)	Counterpremise	− (minus)

For very large increases or decreases, a very large majority or very small minority, and so on, double the symbol. For example, for a very large increase in the number of employees, you could write ↑↑ # emp.

For the profit formula, do write out the whole formula even if the argument mentions only profit, or only profit and either revenues or costs. All three variables go together, and that fact is often the key point for a question that mentions profit.

For any names, unfamiliar "big" words, or other unusual words, use just the first letter of the name or word. In traditional note taking, that wouldn't be adequate, but remember that you only need your map for about 90 seconds. You'll remember a single-letter abbreviation for 90 seconds.

MANHATTAN
PREP

Exercise: Mapping the Argument

Give yourself about one minute to create a map for these arguments from Chapter 1, incorporating the techniques you've learned in this chapter.

1. Budget Fitness will grow its membership base by 10% in the next six months. Budget Fitness has recently crafted a clever ad campaign that it plans to air on several local radio stations.

2. Last year, the Hudson Family Farm was not profitable. However, the farm will be profitable this year. The farm operators have planted cotton, rather than corn, in several fields. Because cotton prices are expected to rise dramatically this year, the farm can expect larger revenues from cotton sales than it previously earned from corn.

Answers can be found on page 48

Answer Key

Below are sample maps for the two given arguments. Your map might differ quite a bit from the samples shown below. That's fine as long as your map accomplishes the following purposes:

- It clearly delineates a conclusion (if there is one).

- It demonstrates the "flow" of information (how one piece of info relates to the next, where applicable)

- It indicates contrasts or changes of direction.

1. Budget Fitness will grow its membership base by 10% in the next six months. Budget Fitness has recently crafted a clever ad campaign that it plans to air on several local radio stations.

Sample 1	BF new ad camp to air → BF member ↑ 10% in 6 mo Ⓒ
Sample 2	ⒸBF mbrs > 10% 6 mos
	↑ BF to put new ads on radio

In this argument, the conclusion was in the first sentence, so you may write down that info before you know that it is the conclusion. The second sentence actually leads to the first sentence, so if you have room to do so on your scrap paper, add that information to the left of the conclusion that you've already written down. In this case, you might end up with something that looks like Sample 1. Alternatively, you might write down each "big idea" on its own line, and then use an arrow to show that the second line leads to the first one, similar to Sample 2.

In both cases, label the conclusion clearly once you've found it.

2. Last year, the Hudson Family Farm was not profitable. However, the farm will be profitable this year. The farm operators have planted cotton, rather than corn, in several fields. Because cotton prices are expected to rise dramatically this year, the farm can expect larger revenues from cotton sales than it previously earned from corn.

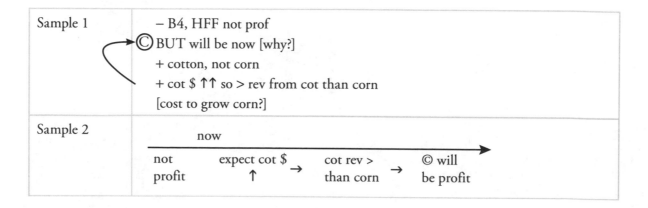

MANHATTAN
PREP

In Sample 1, a "plus" indicates a premise: something the author is using to support the conclusion. A "minus" indicates a counterpremise: something that does not support the conclusion.

Sample 2 shows a timeline. If you've got a future prediction, along with some past background info, a timeline can effectively show the sequence of events. The first two sentences indicate a past/future situation in this argument, so you can tell at the beginning that a timeline might work.

2

Notice the [brackets] in Sample 1. As you make your map, you might also want to jot down what you're thinking. It wasn't profitable before, but it will be now? Why? You're already thinking about that as you continue to read the argument. Later, the argument says the farmers can earn more *revenue* from the cotton, but the conclusion said something about profits. Profit equals revenue minus costs. You've been given some evidence that the farmers may be able to make more money from cotton (and even that's debatable), but you've been told nothing about costs, so how can the argument conclude anything about profits?

The argument indicated that cotton prices are going up; it follows then, that farmers will make more money on the same amount of cotton this year than they did on the same amount of *cotton* last year. How do the prices of cotton and corn compare? Who knows? It's entirely possible that cotton prices have increased but are still lower than corn prices. That's a subtle point, but if you noticed it, you could have jotted down a note so that you wouldn't forget it.

Cheat Sheet

Methodology Cheat Sheet

Identify
the Question

> You'll learn how to do this in later chapters.
>
> The question type indicates what kind of information you can expect to find in the argument and what kind of reasoning will help to answer the question.

Deconstruct
the Argument

> Break the argument down into its building blocks.
>
> Make a very abbreviated map showing both the details and the "flow" of the information.

State the **Goal**

> Very briefly articulate your goal based upon this question type (again, you'll learn the goals for each type in later chapters).

Work from
Wrong to **Right**

> Plan to go through the answers twice.
>
> On the first pass, focus on eliminating anything that is definitely wrong; leave everything else in.
>
> On the second pass, compare any choices that remain, then pick.

Know how you're going to keep track of your answers on your scrap paper. First, decide whether to have a separate ABCDE grid for each problem or whether to use the "write once per page" method described earlier in the chapter. Second, make sure you have four consistent symbols for these four labels:

1. Definitely wrong

2. Maybe

3. I have no idea

4. This is it!

MANHATTAN
PREP

Problem Set

Read the argument and identify the role of each sentence or major piece of information. Make a map for the argument. Use that information to write out the building block structure.

1. A series of research studies has reported that flaxseed oil can have a beneficial effect in reducing tumor growth in mice, particularly the kind of tumor found in human postmenopausal breast cancer. Thus, flaxseed oil should be recommended as an addition to the diets of all postmenopausal women.

2. During the past 30 years, the percentage of the population that smokes cigarettes has consistently declined. During the same time period, however, the number of lung cancer deaths attributed to smoking cigarettes has increased.

3. The Chinese white dolphin is a territorial animal that rarely strays far from its habitat in the Pearl River Delta. In recent years, increasing industrial and agricultural runoff to the delta's waters has caused many white dolphins to perish before they reach breeding age. Unless legislation is enacted to ensure there is no further decline in the delta's water quality, the Chinese white dolphin will become extinct.

4. Most doctors recommend consuming alcohol only in moderation, since the excessive intake of alcohol has been linked to several diseases of the liver. Drinking alcohol is no more dangerous for the liver, however, than abstaining from alcohol entirely. Last year, more nondrinkers than drinkers were diagnosed with liver failure.

5. To increase the productivity of the country's workforce, the government should introduce new food guidelines that recommend a vegetarian diet. A study of thousands of men and women revealed that those who stick to a vegetarian diet have IQs that are approximately five points higher than those who regularly eat meat. The vegetarians were also more likely to have earned advanced degrees and hold high-paying jobs.

Solutions

Note: The sample maps shown below represent one style of map. Just make sure that your map is legible and concise, and that it conveys the main points in a way that makes sense to you.

1.

Argument	Thoughts	Paper
A series of research studies has reported that flaxseed oil can have a beneficial effect in reducing tumor growth in mice, particularly the kind of tumor found in human postmenopausal breast cancer.	*This is a fact. It's either background or a premise.*	Res: Flax helps ↓ tumor mice esp postmen b-cancer
Thus, flaxseed oil should be recommended as an addition to the diets of all postmenopausal women.	*Definitely the conclusion.*	Ⓒ postmen women shd take flax

The structure of this argument is **Premise – Conclusion**.

2.

Argument	Thoughts	Paper
During the past 30 years, the percentage of the population that smokes cigarettes has consistently declined.	*This is a fact. It's either background or a premise.*	30y: % pop smoke cig ↓ steady
During the same time period, however, the number of lung cancer deaths attributed to smoking cigarettes has increased.	*Another fact, so another premise. There isn't a conclusion.*	same time: lung canc dead from cig ↑

The structure of this argument is **Premise – Premise**. Remember, not all GMAT arguments contain conclusions.

2

3.

Argument	Thoughts	Paper
The Chinese white dolphin is a territorial animal that rarely strays far from its habitat in the Pearl River Delta.	*This is a fact. It's either background or a premise.*	Dolphin stays in delta
In recent years, increasing industrial and agricultural runoff to the delta's waters has caused many white dolphins to perish before they reach breeding age.	*This is also a fact—either background or premise.*	Recent: ind + ag in delta → dolphin dies b4 breed
Unless legislation is enacted to ensure there is no further decline in the delta's water quality, the Chinese white dolphin will become extinct.	*And here's the conclusion.* *[Note: H2O here is an abbreviation for water, based on the chemical formula H_2O.]*	IF govt doesn't fix H2O → dolphin extinct

The structure of this argument is **Premise – Premise – Conclusion**.

4.

Argument	Thoughts	Paper
Most doctors recommend consuming alcohol only in moderation, since the excessive intake of alcohol has been linked to several diseases of the liver.	*This is a fact. It's either background or a premise.*	Drs rec ↓ alc bc ↑ alc → liver dis
Drinking alcohol is no more dangerous for the liver, however, than abstaining from alcohol entirely.	*Oh, this has the word "however!" The last sentence was a counter-premise, and this one sounds like the conclusion.*	Ⓒ drink not worse than abstain
Last year, more nondrinkers than drinkers were diagnosed with liver failure.	*This supports the previous sentence; it's a premise. (It also seems pretty flawed. What **percentage** of nondrinkers vs. drinkers had liver disease?)*	Last yr: more nondrink had liv dis

The structure of this argument is **Counterpremise – Conclusion – Premise**.

MANHATTAN
PREP

5.

Argument	Thoughts	Paper
To increase the productivity of the country's workforce, the government should introduce new food guidelines that recommend a vegetarian diet.	*This is definitely a claim. It sounds like a conclusion, though I don't know for sure yet.*	Govt shd rec veg to ↑ wrkr prod
A study of thousands of men and women revealed that those who stick to a vegetarian diet have IQs that are approximately five points higher than those who regularly eat meat.	*This is a fact—the results of a study. It also supports the claim above, so it's a premise.*	Study: veg ↑ IQ than non-veg
The vegetarians were also more likely to have earned advanced degrees and hold high-paying jobs.	*This is another premise supporting the first sentence.*	Veg > better schl + high pay

The structure of this argument is **Conclusion – Premise – Premise**.

Tip: When first learning this method, many people write too much. As part of your review, ask yourself, "Did I write this down in the most effective way? Did my map make sense? Did I write down something that I could have skipped, or did I use too many words when I could have abbreviated more?" If you were really off the mark, write out the map again in a more ideal way—and articulate to yourself why this new way is better than the old way.

Chapter 3

of Critical Reasoning

Structure-Based Family

In This Chapter...

Describe the Role

Describe the Argument

Chapter 3

Structure-Based Family

In the first two chapters, you examined the building blocks of arguments and learned the four-step approach for tackling any Critical Reasoning question:

Step 1: Identify the question.

Step 2: Deconstruct the argument.

Step 3: State the Goal.

Step 4: Work from wrong to right.

Now, you're going to begin tackling the first of the three main Critical Reasoning families: the Structure-Based questions. As the name implies, these questions depend on your ability to understand the structure of the argument. What kinds of building blocks are present in the argument? What role does each building block play?

There are two main Structure question types: **Describe the Role** and **Describe the Argument**.

Describe the Role

Of the two types, Describe the Role is more common. These problems present a standard argument, with one or two portions in **boldface** font. You are asked to describe the *role* that each portion of boldface font plays.

"Role" is just another term for concepts you already know. A bolded portion could be a premise, a conclusion, a counterpremise, an intermediate conclusion, or background information. It could also be a counterconclusion or opposing conclusion, which goes against the author's main conclusion. You might think of this as the final claim of the *other* side of the argument.

These question types are easy to identify, because one or (usually) two statements will be presented in boldface font, and the question stem will include the word *boldface*.

You're going to learn two methods to determine the role of each boldface statement. The Primary Method will always work, but it may be a little more complicated and time-consuming to use. The Secondary Method will allow you to narrow down the answer choices more easily but may not get you all the way to one answer—that is, you may have to guess from a narrowed set of answers.

Primary Method

Classify each statement in boldface as one of the following three things:

1. (C) The author's CONCLUSION.

2. (P) A PREMISE (it supports the author's conclusion)

3. (X) SOMETHING ELSE (maybe a counterpremise, background information, acknowledgement of a weakness in the argument …)

In your notes, you'll classify each statement using the labels C, P, or X, as described above. When you evaluate the answer choices, you'll look for language that matches your labels.

Try this example:

> CEO: Now that Apex Corporation has begun to compete in our market, investors are expecting us to cut our prices to maintain market share. I don't believe this is necessary, however, because the market is growing rapidly and **a certain percentage of customers will always pay more for high-quality products**.
>
> In the argument above, the portion in boldface plays which of the following roles?

How does this argument work? First, the CEO states that investors are expecting a certain action, but she disagrees. She then provides two pieces of evidence intended to support her opinion: the market is growing and some number of customers are willing to pay higher prices. The boldface portion, then, is a premise: it supports the CEO's conclusion that the company does not need to cut prices in order to maintain market share.

Next, look for a P among the answer choices, which tend to be written in a difficult, abstract style. For example, some answers might read:

(A) The statement is evidence that has been used to weaken a claim made by the argument.

(B) The statement has been used to support a claim made by the argument.

(C) The statement is the primary claim made in the argument.

MANHATTAN
PREP

Start with the most basic piece: a building block. The word *claim* is typically a synonym for the conclusion. The first answer says that the statement weakens the conclusion. Something used to weaken the conclusion is a counterpremise; such a statement would be labeled X, not P. Choice (A) is not the correct answer.

The second answer talks about something that *supports a claim*. Since the claim is the conclusion, this answer choice does indeed describe a P, or premise, supporting the conclusion. This is probably the correct answer, but check choice (C) just to make sure.

The third answer describes the conclusion itself, not a premise supporting the conclusion. This choice is incorrect, so choice (**B**) is the correct answer.

If you can use the above method accurately, you will be able to eliminate the four wrong answers and get to the right answer. You might take too much time to do so, though, because of the strange format of the answers (and don't forget that the official questions typically have two boldface statements, not just one). The Secondary Method, as outlined below, may allow you to get rid of some answers more quickly:

Secondary Method
Answer these three questions: 1. Is the statement a FACT or an OPINION? 2. Is the statement FOR or AGAINST the conclusion? 3. If there are two statements, are they on the SAME side of the fence or OPPOSITE sides?

Strategy Tip: Check for the conclusion first. And you can use the same side/opposite side trick with the Primary Method, too: C's and P's are on one side, while X's are on the other.

As with the Primary Method, you then look in the answer choices for matching language. How would this method work on the problem from above? The boldface statement is an OPINION (she hasn't cited actual evidence from customers to support the claim). In addition, the statement is FOR the conclusion. The problem had only one statement, so the third question doesn't apply.

Next, check the answer choices. The word "evidence" typically indicates a fact, not an opinion, so answer (A) is likely incorrect. Answers (B) and (C) both describe claims, or opinions, and both are for the conclusion, so the alternate method wouldn't necessarily allow you to choose between the two. (In this case, you might notice the distinction between a conclusion and a premise and be able to choose the correct answer. This problem, though, is on the easier side.)

Common Trap Answers

The most tempting trap answers on Role questions tend to be "off" by just one word, often at the end of the sentence. For instance, imagine that you've decided the first boldface is a premise in support of the author's conclusion. A tempting wrong answer might read:

(A) The first **[boldface statement]** provides evidence in support of the position that the argument seeks to reject.

Every word of that answer matches what you want to find with the exception of the very last word, *reject*. In fact, if you changed that one word, the answer would be correct:

(A) The first **[boldface statement]** provides evidence in support of the position that the argument seeks to establish.

The first version of the answer choice says that the first boldface is a premise in support of some *counter*conclusion. That's not the kind of premise you want! Read every word carefully, all the way to the end of each answer choice.

Putting It All Together

Try a full example:

Mathematician: Recently, Zubin Ghosh made headlines when he was recognized to have solved the Hilbert Conjecture. Ghosh posted his work on the internet, rather than submitting it to established journals. In fact, **he has no job, let alone a university position**; he lives alone and has refused all acclaim. In reporting on Ghosh, the press unfortunately has reinforced the popular view that mathematicians are antisocial loners. But **mathematicians clearly form a tightly knit community**, frequently collaborating on important efforts; indeed, teams of researchers are working together to extend Ghosh's findings.

In the argument above, the two portions in boldface play which of the following roles?

(A) The first is an observation the author makes to illustrate a social pattern; the second is a generalization of that pattern.

(B) The first is evidence in favor of the popular view expressed in the argument; the second is a brief restatement of that view.

(C) The first is a specific example of a generalization that the author contradicts; the second is a reiteration of that generalization.

(D) The first is a specific counterexample to a generalization that the author asserts; the second is that generalization.

(E) The first is a judgment that counters the primary assertion expressed in the argument; the second is a circumstance on which that judgment is based.

Step 1: Identify the question.

In the argument above, the two portions in boldface play which of the following roles?	*This is a Role question. The argument contains bold font, and the question stem contains the words "boldface" and "role."*	R A B C D E

Step 2: Deconstruct the argument.

Mathematician: Recently, Zubin Ghosh made headlines when he was recognized to have solved the Hilbert Conjecture.	*A past fact—this is likely background. Still, jot down a note.*	M: Ghosh solved conjecture
Ghosh simply posted his work on the Internet, rather than submitting it to established journals.	*Sounds like more background.*	posted on Int
In fact, **he has no job, let alone a university position**; he lives alone and has refused all acclaim.	*Here's the first boldface. He's not a mathematician; that's surprising. Still, I don't know what the conclusion is, so I don't know what role this sentence is playing.*	No job
In reporting on Ghosh, the press unfortunately has reinforced the popular view that mathematicians are antisocial loners.	*So the first boldface is "evidence" of "the popular view" that mathematicians are loners…but the sentence also uses the word "unfortunately" so it sounds like the author doesn't agree…*	Press: math = loners
But **mathematicians clearly form a tightly knit community**, frequently collaborating on important efforts; indeed, teams of researchers are working together to extend Ghosh's findings.	*I was right; the author disagrees. The author's conclusion is this second boldface statement, so I can label it with a Ⓒ.*	ⒸBUT math = commun, collab
	Now, what about that first boldface statement? It's not the conclusion, and it doesn't support the conclusion, so it must be an X: Something Else.	R A B C D E Ghosh solved conjecture posted on Int ⓍNo job Press: math = loners ⒸBUT math = commun, collab

Step 3: State the goal.

The first boldface statement is an X; that is, it is neither the conclusion nor a premise. In this case, it supports the alternate point of view, so call it a counterpremise. It goes against the conclusion. The second boldface statement is a C; it is the author's conclusion.

Remind yourself:

> In the right answer, the first statement will be consistent with an X label and the second statement will be consistent with a C label. I'm looking for an XC combo, and those two labels are on "opposite sides."

Step 4: Work from wrong to right.

(A) The first is an observation the author makes to illustrate a social pattern; the second is a generalization of that pattern.	*Hmm. I'm not 100% sure what they mean by "illustrate a social pattern," but the description of the two statements here makes them sound like they're on the same "side"—the first illustrates something, and the second generalizes that same thing. I want an "opposite sides" answer.*	A
(B) The first is evidence in favor of the popular view expressed in the argument; the second is a brief restatement of that view.	*The first supports a popular view…okay, maybe. You could call the press view the popular view. Oh, but then it says that the second restates that same view. These two are on the same side again, and I want an "opposite sides" answer.*	B
(C) The first is a specific example of a generalization that the author contradicts; the second is a reiteration of that generalization.	*"The first is a <something> that the author contradicts." The <something> part confuses me, but I agree that the author contradicts the first one; this is a good description of a "label X" statement. Hmm. The second repeats "that generalization"—the same one mentioned in the first statement? No, I'm looking for opposite sides, not a repetition.*	C̶
(D) The first is a specific counter-example to a generalization that the author asserts; the second is that generalization.	*The first is a counterexample to something the author says? Yes, that accurately describes a "label X." The second is "that generalization" I crossed off the last one for this same language. But wait…which generalization is this referring to this time? Oh, a generalization that the author asserts; that's the conclusion, which is a "label C." Leave this answer in.*	D̲

| (E) The first is a judgment that counters the primary assertion expressed in the argument; the second is a circumstance on which that judgment is based. | *"Counters" language—yes, the first statement does counter the conclusion, which is consistent with the label X. "That judgment" = the first boldface. The second is not something on which the first one is based—that would be same side, and I want opposite sides.* | E |

A   B   C̶   Ⓓ   E̶

The correct answer is (**D**).

Common Trap Answers

Half Right

The test writers try to set some traps for you on incorrect Describe the Role answers. For example, one of the descriptions might match one of the boldface statements, but the other one won't match. Several of the wrong answers in the last problem were **Half Right** in this way.

One Word Off

In addition, a very tricky trap answer might be wrong by just one word; we call this the **One Word Off** trap. For example, you might be looking for a premise that supports the conclusion. The answer choice might say, "The first boldface supports a claim that the argument as a whole argues against."

What does that really mean? This choice says that the boldface supports a counterconclusion, not the author's conclusion—but you wouldn't know until you read the very last word of the sentence. In fact, if you changed the word "against" to the word "for," then the choice would be describing a premise in support of the conclusion!

Describe the Argument

Describe the Argument questions can be similar to Role questions: both often offer "abstract" answer choices based on the *structure* of the argument, perhaps referring to the various building blocks (conclusions, premises, and so on). The majority of these Argument questions will offer two competing points of view in a dialogue format. Then you might be asked how the second person responds to the first person's argument.

Important note: other question types can also be presented in this "two people speaking" format—the mere existence of two speakers does not make the problem a Describe the Argument problem. *Always identify the question type using the question stem.*

A minority of these questions will offer just one point of view and ask you how the author of that argument develops his or her point of view.

Common question formulations include:

> Baram responds to Sadie's argument by …

> Baram challenges Sadie's argument by …

> The author develops the argument by doing which of the following?

These all indicate that you have a Describe the Argument question.

Your task is to determine how a particular part of the text was constructed. When the text is a dialogue between two people, then read and deconstruct the first person's complete argument just as you would do for any other GMAT argument. Next, examine the response and figure out which piece of the argument the response attacks.

Try an example:

> Baram: I need to learn the names of 100 muscles for the anatomy exam in two hours. I've just memorized 5 of them in 5 minutes, so I only need 95 more minutes to study. Therefore, I'll have plenty of time to memorize everything and get a perfect score on the test.

> Sadie: Are you sure? Perhaps the more you memorize, the harder it gets.

> Sadie responds to Baram by

What is Baram's argument? What is his conclusion, and how does he support it?

> must learn 100 names in 2h
>
> mem 5 in 5m, so need 95m
>
> © will get 100%

Which part does Sadie attack? Does she attack the conclusion directly? No, but her words certainly cast doubt on Baram's eventual conclusion. She attacks Baram's assumption that he can maintain the same rate of learning, 1 name every minute, for all 100 words. He doesn't explicitly state that he can maintain that rate, but he clearly believes it to be true. The correct answer might be something like:

> **Sadie calls into question an assumption Baram makes about the efficacy of his plan.**

This answer addresses the appropriate part of the argument—an assumption that Baram makes about his plan. An incorrect answer might look something like:

> **Sadie introduces new evidence that contradicts one of Baram's premises.**

Sadie does say something new, but does it rise to the level of evidence? She only suggests that his memorization rate might not be constant; she doesn't prove that it is not. While you might be able to argue that the word "evidence" is okay, the word "contradicts" clearly takes things too far. Sadie does not definitively contradict Baram's premise that he will need only 95 more minutes; rather, she raises a question as to *whether* he can memorize the words in only 95 minutes.

Ultimately, the attack is designed to find fault with the conclusion, but don't assume that the second person is attacking the conclusion directly. Tearing down any piece of the argument would ultimately undermine the conclusion, so find the piece that the second person most directly attacks.

You probably won't be able to anticipate the exact wording of the correct answer, but if you can identify the part of the argument addressed, then you are in a much better position to identify the appropriate "matching" language in the correct answer.

Try a full example:

> Mayor: The recycling program costs us nearly $1 million to operate every year, and our budget shortfall this year is projected to be $5 million. Cutting the recycling program will help balance the budget.
>
> Consumer Advocate: It costs the city more to throw something out than to recycle it.
>
> The consumer advocate responds to the mayor by

(A)   establishing that the mayor's figures were incorrectly calculated
(B)   accepting the mayor's conclusion but questioning the legality of the plan
(C)   interpreting the mayor's evidence in a way that reduces the validity of the mayor's claim
(D)   introducing a new piece of information that calls into question the validity of the mayor's conclusion
(E)   pointing out that the mayor has not adequately considered the potential causes and effects of the budget shortfall

Step 1: Identify the question.

The consumer advocate responds to the mayor by	*This is a Describe the Argument question. Two people are talking, and I have to explain how one responds to the other.*	DA A B C D E

Step 2: Deconstruct the argument.

Mayor: The recycling program costs us nearly $1 million to operate every year, and our budget shortfall this year is projected to be $5 million.	*The mayor is stating a couple of facts—recycling costs $1m and they're going to miss their budget by $5m.*	M: Recyc cost $1m; this yr $5m short
Cutting the recycling program will help balance the budget.	*So the mayor suggests that they cut the R program in order to help balance the budget.*	→ cut R → bal budg Ⓒ
Consumer Advocate: It costs the city more to throw something out than to recycle it.	*That's interesting. The advocate says that it costs even more to throw something out. Why does this matter? If you can't recycle something, what are you going to do with it instead? Probably throw it out.*	Advoc: Throw away costs > R

Step 3: State the goal.

For Describe the Argument questions, you have to address how some part of the argument is made: in this case, how the consumer advocate responds to the mayor. First, it sounds as if the advocate thinks that the mayor's plan isn't going to work since the advocate says that throwing stuff out is more costly than recycling it. If that's true, then the plan to cut the recycling program just got a bit worse—it might not actually achieve the ultimate goal, which is to save money and balance the budget.

State your goal briefly to yourself before going to the answers:

> *The answer I find should indicate that the consumer advocate disagrees with the mayor specifically questioning whether the suggested action (cutting the recycling program) will result in the desired outcome (saving money, helping to balance the budget).*

Step 4: Work from wrong to right.

(A) establishing that the mayor's figures were incorrectly calculated	*The consumer advocate doesn't say anything about the mayor's figures—in fact, the advocate doesn't dispute the mayor's evidence at all. Rather, the advocate attacks the mayor's assumption that cutting the program will lead to balancing the budget.*	A̶
(B) accepting the mayor's conclusion but questioning the legality of the plan	*The advocate doesn't accept the conclusion, nor does the advocate say anything about legality. Rather, the advocate questions whether the plan will really lead to saving money.*	B̶
(C) interpreting the mayor's evidence in a way that reduces the validity of the mayor's claim	*Hmm. Maybe. The advocate does reduce the validity of the mayor's claim. I'm not 100% sure what "interpreting the evidence" means. I'll leave this in for now.*	C̲
(D) introducing a new piece of information that calls into question the validity of the mayor's conclusion	*The advocate does call the mayor's conclusion into question, yes. Oh, I see—this one is better than answer (C) because the advocate does introduce a new piece of info (that it costs more to throw something away).*	C̶ D̲
(E) pointing out that the mayor has not adequately considered the potential causes and effects of the budget shortfall	*This one is tricky. It's true that the mayor hasn't fully considered the potential effects of the plan to cut the recycling program—but that's not what this choice says. It talks about the causes and effects of the budget shortfall.*	E̶

A̶   B̶   C̶   Ⓓ   E̶

The correct answer is (**D**).

Common Trap Answers

One Word Off

The most tempting trap answers on Describe the Argument questions are similar to those on Role questions: most of the answer is fine, but one or two words will throw the answer off.

In addition, because most of these arguments will consist of a second person objecting to something the first person says, it will always be tempting to choose an answer that indicates that, for example, the consumer advocate rejects the mayor's conclusion. The advocate's comment does weaken the mayor's conclusion, but it may not directly attack the conclusion—and the question asks you to articulate what the advocate directly attacks.

3

Cheat Sheets

Describe the Role Cheat Sheet

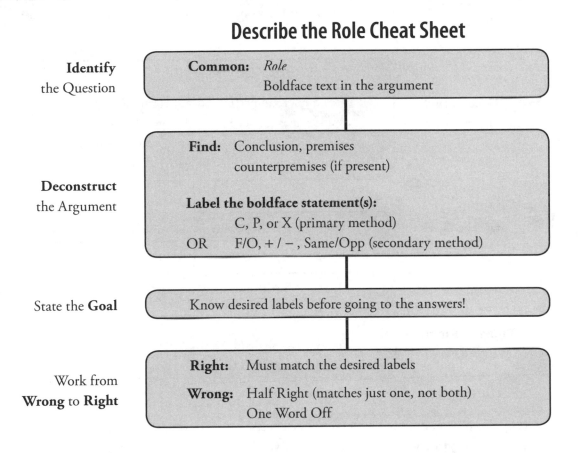

Identify
the Question

Common: *Role*
Boldface text in the argument

Deconstruct
the Argument

Find: Conclusion, premises
counterpremises (if present)

Label the boldface statement(s):
C, P, or X (primary method)
OR   F/O, + / − , Same/Opp (secondary method)

State the **Goal**

Know desired labels before going to the answers!

Work from
Wrong to **Right**

Right: Must match the desired labels

Wrong: Half Right (matches just one, not both)
One Word Off

Photocopy this page and keep it with the review sheets you're creating as you study. Better yet, use this page as a guide to create your own review sheet—you'll remember the material better if you write it down yourself.

3

Describe the Argument Cheat Sheet

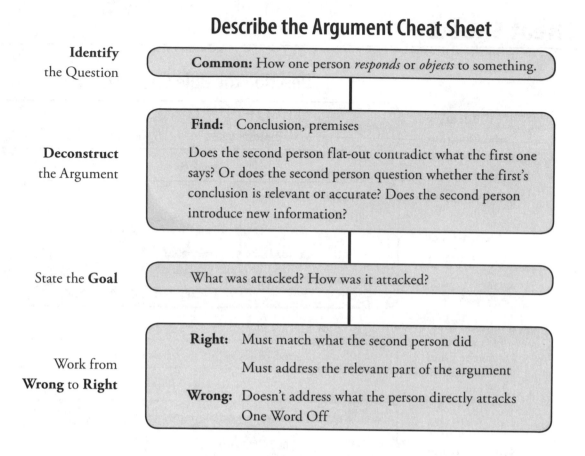

Identify
the Question

Common: How one person *responds* or *objects* to something.

Deconstruct
the Argument

Find: Conclusion, premises

Does the second person flat-out contradict what the first one says? Or does the second person question whether the first's conclusion is relevant or accurate? Does the second person introduce new information?

State the **Goal**

What was attacked? How was it attacked?

Work from
Wrong to **Right**

Right: Must match what the second person did

Must address the relevant part of the argument

Wrong: Doesn't address what the person directly attacks
One Word Off

Photocopy this page and keep it with the review sheets you're creating as you study. Better yet, use this page as a guide to create your own review sheet—you'll remember the material better if you write it down yourself.

MANHATTAN
PREP

Problem Set

1. *Ad Revenues*

    Media Critic: Network executives allege that television viewership is decreasing due to the availability of television programs on other platforms, such as the internet and mobile devices. These executives claim that **declining viewership will cause advertising revenue to fall and networks will thus be unable to spend the large sums necessary to produce high-quality programming**. That development, in turn, will lead to a dearth of programming for the very devices that cannibalized television's audience. However, research shows that users of alternative platforms are exposed to new programs and, **as a result, actually increase the number of hours per week that they watch television**. This demonstrates that alternative platforms will not prevent networks from increasing advertising revenue.

    The portions in boldface play which of the following roles in the media critic's argument?

    (A) The first is a trend that weighs against the critic's claim; the second is that claim.

    (B) The first is a prediction that is challenged by the argument; the second is a finding upon which the argument depends.

    (C) The first clarifies the reasoning behind the critic's claim; the second demonstrates why that claim is flawed.

    (D) The first acknowledges a position that the network executives accept as true; the second is a consequence of that position.

    (E) The first opposes the critic's claim through an analogy; the second outlines a scenario in which that claim will not hold.

2. *Renaissance Masters*

Many people praise High Renaissance painting for creating very realistic images from observation, but **scholars have documented that some High Renaissance painters used pinhole cameras to project the likeness of their subjects onto the canvas and painted from there**. Thus, people who credit High Renaissance painters with superior artistic skills are misguided. **Painting from a projected image requires only an insignificant amount of additional skill beyond that needed to copy a picture outright.**

In the argument given, the two boldfaced portions play which of the following roles?

(A) The first is a finding that has been used to support a conclusion that the argument rejects; the second is a claim that supports that conclusion.

(B) The first is a finding that has been used to support a conclusion that the argument rejects; the second is that conclusion.

(C) The first is a claim put forth to support a conclusion that the argument rejects; the second is a consideration that is introduced to counter the force of that evidence.

(D) The first is evidence that forms the basis for the position that the argument seeks to establish; the second is a claim presented to solidify that position.

(E) The first is evidence that forms the basis for the position that the argument seeks to establish; the second is that position.

3. *Democracy*

As the United States demonstrated during its early development, it is not enough for citizens simply to have rights; the successful functioning of a democracy requires that they also know how to exercise those rights. Access to formal education was one necessary component that helped the U.S. citizenry learn how to exercise its rights. Therefore, in order for a democracy to function successfully, its citizens must have access to a formal education.

The author develops the argument by

(A) using an analogy to establish a precedent for a planned future event

(B) illustrating differences in the requirements for the functioning of a democracy depending upon the democracy in question

(C) introducing an example that illustrates a common principle

(D) forming a hypothesis that explains apparently contradictory pieces of evidence

(E) supplying an alternate explanation for a known phenomenon

MANHATTAN
PREP

4. *Malaria*

In an attempt to explain the cause of malaria, a deadly infectious disease, early European settlers in Hong Kong attributed the malady to poisonous gases supposedly emanating from low-lying swampland. In the 1880s, however, doctors determined that Anopheles mosquitoes were responsible for transmitting the disease to humans after observing that **the female of the species can carry a parasitic protozoan that is passed on to unsuspecting humans when a mosquito feasts on a person's blood**.

What function does the statement in boldface fulfill with respect to the argument presented above?

(A) It provides support for the explanation of a particular phenomenon.

(B) It presents evidence that contradicts an established fact.

(C) It offers confirmation of a contested assumption.

(D) It identifies the cause of an erroneous conclusion.

(E) It proposes a new conclusion in place of an earlier conjecture.

5. *Digital Marketing*

Sania: The newest workers in the workforce are the most effective digital marketing employees because they are more likely to use social networking websites and tools themselves.

Carlos: But effective digital marketing also requires very technical expertise, such as search engine optimization, that is best learned on the job via prolonged exposure and instruction.

Carlos responds to Sania by

(A) demonstrating that Sania's conclusion is based upon evidence that is not relevant to the given situation

(B) questioning the accuracy of the evidence presented by Sania in support of her conclusion

(C) reinforcing Sania's argument by contributing an additional piece of evidence in support of her conclusion

(D) pointing out differences in the qualifications desired by different employers seeking digital marketing employees

(E) providing an additional piece of evidence that undermines a portion of Sania's claim

6. *Innovative Design*

Products with innovative and appealing designs relative to competing products can often command substantially higher prices in the marketplace. **Because design innovations are quickly copied by other manufacturers**, many consumer technology companies charge as much as possible for their new designs to extract as much value as possible from them. But large profits generated by the innovative designs give competitors stronger incentives to copy the designs. Therefore, **the best strategy to maximize overall profit from an innovative new design is to charge less than the greatest possible price**.

In the argument above, the two portions in boldface play which of the following roles?

(A) The first is an assumption that supports a described course of action; the second provides a consideration to support a preferred course of action.

(B) The first is a consideration that helps explain the appeal of a certain strategy; the second presents an alternative strategy endorsed by the argument.

(C) The first is a phenomenon that makes a specific strategy unlikely to be successful; the second is that strategy.

(D) The first is a consideration that demonstrates why a particular approach is flawed; the second describes a way to amend that approach.

(E) The first is a factor used to rationalize a particular strategy; the second is a factor against that strategy.

MANHATTAN
PREP

7. *Gray Wolf Population*

Government representative: Between 1996 and 2005, the gray wolf population in Minnesota grew nearly 50%; the gray wolf population in Montana increased by only 13% during the same period. Clearly, the Minnesota gray wolf population is more likely to survive and thrive long term.

Environmentalist: But the gray wolf population in Montana is nearly 8 times the population in Minnesota; above a certain critical breeding number, the population is stable and does not require growth in order to survive.

The environmentalist challenges the government representative's argument by doing which of the following?

(A) introducing additional evidence that undermines an assumption made by the representative

(B) challenging the representative's definition of a critical breeding number

(C) demonstrating that the critical breeding number of the two wolf populations differs significantly

(D) implying that the two populations of wolves could be combined in order to preserve the species

(E) suggesting that the Montana wolf population grew at a faster rate than stated in the representative's argument

3

Solutions

1. Ad Revenues: The correct answer is **(B)**.

Step 1: Identify the question.

The portions in boldface play which of the following roles in the media critic's argument?	*This is a Role question. The question contains the word "boldface," and I'm asked to find the "role" of each bold statement.*	R A B C D E

Step 2: Deconstruct the argument.

Media Critic: Network executives allege that television viewership is decreasing due to the availability of television programs on other platforms, such as the internet and mobile devices.	*The word "allege" tells me this is a claim. Also, the critic is talking about what other people claim, so I'm guessing the critic is going to contradict what they claim—so this is probably a counterpremise.*	Critic: Execs say TV ↓ b/c use other plats
These executives claim that **declining viewership will cause advertising revenue to fall and networks will thus be unable to spend the large sums necessary to produce high-quality programming**.	*More from the execs. More claims about bad things happening. Is the last thing the execs' conclusion? This is the 1st boldface. If the critic contradicts the execs later, then this first boldface will be labeled an X.*	Execs: TV ↓ → ad ↓ → no $ for qual prog
That development, in turn, will lead to a dearth of programming for the very devices that cannibalized television's audience.	*Ah, I see. Ironic. The fact that people are watching on other platforms will eventually lead to not having enough programming for those other platforms. Conclusion of the execs.*	→ no prog for other plats
However, research shows that users of alternative platforms are exposed to new programs and, **as a result, actually increase the number of hours per week that they watch television**.	*Here's the contradiction! I'll wait till I find the conclusion for sure, but the first boldface is probably an X, which would make this one a premise (P).*	BUT users of alt plats watch MORE TV

3

| This demonstrates that alternative platforms will not prevent networks from increasing advertising revenue. | *Okay, the critic is concluding the opposite: that ad rates will go up. And if that's my conclusion, then the first boldface is indeed an X and the second one supports the critic's conclusion, so it's a P.* | ©ad rates

 Want: X P |

Step 3: State the goal.

The question asks me to find the role of two boldface statements. The critic's conclusion is in the last line, and the second boldface, right before it, supports that conclusion. The second boldface is a premise (P). The first boldface is part of the executives' argument, which is the opposite of the critic's argument, so the first boldface is an X. I want to find the combo X P (in that order) in an answer choice.

Step 4: Work from wrong to right.

(A) The first is a trend that weighs against the critic's claim; the second is that claim.	*"Weighs against the critic's claim"—yes, that's consistent with an X label. The second is "that" claim, meaning the critic's claim. No. The second one is a P, not a C.*	A̶
(B) The first is a prediction that is challenged by the argument; the second is a finding upon which the argument depends.	*That's true, the critic does challenge the first one. That's an X. And the second one is a P, so this could be something upon which the critic argument depends. I'll keep it in.*	B̰
(C) The first clarifies the reasoning behind the critic's claim; the second demonstrates why that claim is flawed.	*Clarifies the critic's claim? No. The first one is something the execs claim. I don't even need to read the second half of the answer.*	C̶
(D) The first acknowledges a position that the network executives accept as true; the second is a consequence of that position.	*Yes, the execs do accept the first boldface as true—it's their premise. And they're on the opposite side of the critic, so something they think is an X. Okay, that's fine. "The second is a consequence of that position." What position? Oh, they use "position" in the first half of the sentence...the execs' position. The second isn't something about the execs' position. It goes against the execs' position. No.*	D̶

MANHATTAN
PREP

(E) The first opposes the critic's claim through an analogy; the second outlines a scenario in which that claim will not hold.	*The first one does oppose what the critic concludes. I'm not quite sure whether it does so "through an analogy." What about the second half? A scenario in which the critic's claim won't hold—meaning something that's on the opposite side of what the critic says. No! The second one outlines a scenario in which the execs' claim won't hold, not the critic's claim.*	E̶

A̶   Ⓑ   C̶   D̶   F̶

2. Renaissance Masters: The correct answer is (**D**).

Step 1: Identify the question.

In the argument given, the two boldfaced portions play which of the following roles?	*The word "boldfaced," along with the boldface font in the argument, indicates that this is a Role question.*	R A B C D E

Step 2: Deconstruct the argument.

Many people praise High Renaissance painting for creating very realistic images from observation,	*The "many people" intro feels like there's a contrast coming…and there is! Okay, just get this piece down first.*	Many like Hi Ren pics b/c realistic
but **scholars have documented that some High Renaissance painters used pinhole cameras to project the likeness of their subjects onto the canvas and painted from there.**	*People think the High Renaissance painters could paint realistically just by observing, but actually some were just projecting the images onto a canvas and sort of tracing the image.*	BUT some painters just projected + traced
Thus, people who credit High Renaissance painters with superior artistic skills are misguided.	*The word "thus" might mean this is the conclusion. The previous sentence only said that "some" painters did the tracing thing, not all of them. But this sentence seems to be condemning all of them.*	People who like Hi Ren = misguided

Painting from a projected image requires only an insignificant amount of additional skill beyond that needed to copy a picture outright.	*Okay, the last sentence was definitely the conclusion. This sentence is supporting the conclusion. If this is true, then yes, painters who use this technique aren't that great.*	project = low skill
	I'm not 100% sure how to label the first boldface, but I did notice that the first one was a fact and the second one was an opinion. I could use the secondary method to solve.	

Step 3: State the goal.

I need to identify the role of the two boldfaced statements as they relate to the conclusion—which was that people who think High Renaissance painters are really skilled are misguided. The first one is a fact, and the second one is an opinion. The first one is FOR the conclusion. So is the second one.

Step 4: Work from wrong to right.

(A) The first is a finding that has been used to support a conclusion that the argument rejects; the second is a claim that supports that conclusion.	*A "finding" could be a fact, and a claim is an opinion, so this one is okay so far.*	A̰
(B) The first is a finding that has been used to support a conclusion that the argument rejects; the second is that conclusion.	*A "finding" could be a fact, and the conclusion is technically an opinion. But the boldface opinion is FOR the conclusion; it's not actually the conclusion itself.*	B̶
(C) The first is a claim put forth to support a conclusion that the argument rejects; the second is a consideration that is introduced to counter the force of that evidence.	*A "claim" is not a fact. I can eliminate this one.*	C̶
(D) The first is evidence that forms the basis for the position that the argument seeks to establish; the second is a claim presented to solidify that position.	*"Evidence" can be a fact, and a claim is an opinion. This one has to stay in, too.*	D̰

MANHATTAN
PREP

(E) The first is evidence that forms the basis for the position that the argument seeks to establish; the second is that position.	*"Evidence" can be a fact, but the second boldface is an opinion supporting the conclusion, while this choice says that the second boldface is the "position," or conclusion. I can eliminate this one.*	E
Compare (A) and (D)	*Based on the fact / opinion technique, I can't get any further; I just have to guess between (A) and (D).* *The main technique can distinguish between (A) and (D): both boldfaces are premises used to support the author's conclusion. Answer (A) says that the first boldface is used "to support a conclusion that the argument rejects." Eliminate answer (A).*	A͟ and D͟

A͟   B   C̶   Ⓓ   E̶

3. Democracy: The correct answer is **(C)**.

Step 1: Identify the question.

The author develops the argument by	*The wording is similar to a Describe the Argument question, though it doesn't have the "two people talking" feature. This might be one of the rare variants that doesn't have two people talking. A quick glance at the abstract wording of the answer choices confirms: this is a Describe Arg question.*	DA A B C D E

Step 2: Deconstruct the argument.

As the United States demonstrated during its early development, it is not enough for citizens simply to have rights; the successful functioning of a democracy requires that they also know how to exercise those rights.	*Okay, specific example of a principle: the US showed that citizens need to have rights AND need to know how to exercise those rights.*	US: not just have rights but know how to exercise → success democ
Access to formal education was one necessary component that helped the US citizenry learn how to exercise its rights.	*More detail on the US example. Access to formal education was needed to know how to exercise those rights.*	Need access to formal educ →
Therefore, in order for a democracy to function successfully, its citizens must have access to a formal education.	*Conclusion. The author's just sort of putting together the two "end" pieces of the argument here.*	Ⓒ Need formal edu for success democ

Step 3: State the goal.

The author concludes that formal education is necessary in general for a democracy to be successful. The evidence: it happened this way in one country (the US).

Step 4: Work from wrong to right.

(A) using an analogy to establish a precedent for a planned future event	*The argument used an example. Is that the same thing as an analogy? Maybe. Oh, but what's the "planned future event"? There isn't anything; rather, the author concluded with a general statement, not a discussion of an event.*	A̶
(B) illustrating differences in the requirements for the functioning of a democracy depending upon the democracy in question	*I can imagine that it would be true that there are different requirements for different governments…but that's not what this argument says. The author only mentions the US and then concludes something in general about that.*	B̶
(C) introducing an example that illustrates a common principle	*This looks decent. The argument did introduce an example and then used that to conclude a general principle.*	C̲

MANHATTAN
PREP

| (D) forming a hypothesis that explains apparently contradictory pieces of evidence | *It would be reasonable to describe the conclusion as a hypothesis… but there aren't any contradictory things in the argument. Rather, the example given does illustrate the conclusion.* | ~~D~~ |
| (E) supplying an alternate explanation for a known phenomenon | *The author doesn't supply an "alternate" explanation; he isn't arguing against anyone. He just concludes something from the US example.* | ~~E~~ |

~~A~~   ~~B~~   Ⓒ   ~~D~~   ~~E~~

4. Malaria: The correct answer is (**A**).

Step 1: Identify the question.

| What function does the statement in boldface fulfill with respect to the argument presented above? | *This is a Role question. The question contains the word "boldface," and I'm asked to find the "function" of each bold statement.* | R   A B C D E |

Step 2: Deconstruct the argument.

| In an attempt to explain the cause of malaria, a deadly infectious disease, early European settlers in Hong Kong attributed the malady to poisonous gases supposedly emanating from low-lying swampland. | *This is a fact. Likely either background or premise.* | Euros in HK: Poison gas → malaria |
| In the 1880s, however, doctors determined that Anopheles mosquitoes were responsible for transmitting the disease to humans after observing that **the female of the species can carry a parasitic protozoan that is passed on to unsuspecting humans when a mosquito feasts on a person's blood.** | *Okay, this is still a fact, but it's the conclusion of the story. They used to think it was one thing, and then they figured out it was really the mosquitoes. The boldface language, in particular, is the evidence used to show that it was mosquitoes. That's a Premise.* | But 1880s MDs: mosq bite, pass parasite blood

Want: P |

Step 3: State the goal.

The question specifically asks me what role this information plays: "the female carries a parasite that is passed to humans when a mosquito bites someone." Because of that, the scientists decided that the mosquitoes were transmitting the disease. That's the most like a P—a premise that supports some further conclusion.

I need to find the abstract language that indicates some kind of premise or support.

Step 4: Work from wrong to right.

(A) It provides support for the explanation of a particular phenomenon.	*"Support"—that's good—for a "phenomenon." Okay, that's just fancy-speak for: provides support for something that happened. That sounds okay. Leave it in.*	A̰
(B) It presents evidence that contradicts an established fact.	*"Evidence"—that's also good. And that evidence does "contradict" what the earlier settlers thought! Oh, wait—was that an established fact? Let me look at the first sentence again. No, they thought that, but the argument doesn't say it was an "established fact." Cross this one off.*	B
(C) It offers confirmation of a contested assumption.	*"Confirmation" is also good…of a "contested assumption." I'm not quite sure what they're referring to when they say "assumption," but nothing was contested here. First, some people thought one thing, and later, new evidence led some doctors to conclude something else. No.*	C̶
(D) It identifies the cause of an erroneous conclusion.	*No—the only thing we might be able to describe as an erroneous conclusion is what the early settlers thought. But the bold stuff supports the doctors' conclusion.*	D̶
(E) It proposes a new conclusion in place of an earlier conjecture.	*Oh, yes, a new conclusion. Yes, that's exactly what the argument says! Oh, wait—I labeled the boldface stuff a P, not a C. Why was that? Oh, I see—tricky. The first half of the sentence, the non-bold part, is the new conclusion. The bold part is the evidence supporting that. This isn't it after all!*	E̶

Ⓐ   B̶   C̶   D̶   E̶

MANHATTAN
PREP

5. Digital Marketing: The correct answer is **(E)**.

Step 1: Identify the question.

Carlos responds to Sania by	*The "two person" structure and the focus on how Carlos responds indicate that this is a Describe the Argument question.*	DA A B C D E

Step 2: Deconstruct the argument.

Sania: The newest workers in the workforce are the most effective digital marketing employees because they are more likely to use social networking websites and tools themselves.	*Sania claims that the workers who use certain online tools are also the most effective at digital marketing, and that those people are the newest workers.*	Sania: new empl use soc nw → most eff dig mktg Ⓒ
Carlos: But effective digital marketing also requires very technical expertise, such as search engine optimization, that is best learned on the job via prolonged exposure and instruction.	*Carlos doesn't dispute Sania's evidence, but he brings up a new point: you also need these other skills to be a good digital marketer…and those skills are learned on the job over a long time ("prolonged")…which hurts Sania's claim that the <u>newest</u> workers are the most effective.*	Carlos But eff dig mktg needs tech expertise, best learned on job

Step 3: State the goal.

I need to articulate <u>how</u> Carlos responds to Sania. He doesn't say that she's wrong about the newest workers using social networking tools. Rather, he says that digital marketers also need this other skill that takes a long time to learn on the job. If that's the case, this weakens Sania's claim that the <u>newest</u> workers are the most effective.

Step 4: Work from wrong to right.

(A) demonstrating that Sania's conclusion is based upon evidence that is not relevant to the given situation	*Carlos doesn't say anything negative about Sania's evidence; rather, he introduces new evidence that attacks Sania's assumption that her piece of evidence is the most important thing to consider.*	A̶
(B) questioning the accuracy of the evidence presented by Sania in support of her conclusion	*This is similar to choice (A); Carlos doesn't question Sania's evidence.*	B̶
(C) reinforcing Sania's argument by contributing an additional piece of evidence in support of her conclusion	*Carlos does contribute an additional piece of evidence, but his new evidence hurts Sania's argument. Carlos doesn't support Sania's conclusion.*	C̶
(D) pointing out differences in the qualifications desired by different employers seeking digital marketing employees	*Carlos does point out a different way to assess the effectiveness of digital marketing employees, but he doesn't mention employers at all or differences among different employers.*	D̶
(E) providing an additional piece of evidence that undermines a portion of Sania's claim	*Bingo. This is exactly what Carlos does—a new piece of information that hurts the "newest workers" portion of Sania's claim.*	Ḛ

A̶   B̶   C̶   D̶   Ⓔ

6. Innovative Design: The correct answer is **(B)**.

Step 1: Identify the question.

In the argument above, the two portions in boldface play which of the following roles?	*This is a Role question. The question contains the word "boldface," and I'm asked to find the "role" of each bold statement.*	R A B C D E

Step 2: Deconstruct the argument.

Products with innovative and appealing designs relative to competing products can often command substantially higher prices in the marketplace.	*Sort of between a fact and a claim. Probably a premise.*	Innov designs → ↑↑ $

MANHATTAN
PREP

Because design innovations are quickly copied by other manufacturers, many consumer technology companies charge as much as possible for their new designs to extract as much value as possible from them.	*Getting more towards claim-based material, with the first half of the sentence providing support for the second half. I'm not sure yet whether this is the conlusion though.*	Because others copy many co's charge ↑↑ $
But large profits generated by the innovative designs give competitors stronger incentives to copy the designs.	*BUT signals a contrast. Oh, so there's actually a drawback to making a lot of money: competitors will copy even faster so I guess that could hurt market share. That's interesting.*	BUT ↑↑ prof → incent to copy
Therefore, **the best strategy to maximize overall profit from an innovative new design is to charge less than the greatest possible price**.	*Here we go, the conclusion. The person's claiming that companies actually <u>shouldn't</u> charge the largest possible price and this will actually help maximize profits in the end. The second boldface is the conclusion; that gets a C. The first boldface is a premise that supports a strategy the argument disagrees with (that companies should charge the greatest possible price for an ID).*	Ⓒ to max prof charge < than max price Want: X C

Step 3: State the goal.

The question asks me to determine the role played by each of two boldface statements. I've decided the second one is the conclusion and the first is a premise supporting an alternate strategy, so I want to find an answer that gives this combo: X C (in that order).

Step 4: Work from wrong to right.

(A) The first is an assumption that supports a described course of action; the second provides a consideration to support a preferred course of action.	*Hmm, they call the first an assumption, not a premise, but I suppose that's okay; they do say it "supports" something. The second, though, is the actual conclusion—but this answer choice makes the second sound like another premise. I don't think so.*	A̶
(B) The first is a consideration that helps explain the appeal of a certain strategy; the second presents an alternative strategy endorsed by the argument.	*The wording for the first statement is a little strange, but I suppose that could be considered a premise. And, it does support the greatest possible price strategy. The second boldface is the strategy the argument supports. Keep this one.*	B̰
(C) The first is a phenomenon that makes a specific strategy unlikely to be successful; the second is that strategy.	*The first boldface provides support for the first strategy. It definitely doesn't weaken the author's strategy. Eliminate this answer choice.*	C̶
(D) The first is a consideration that demonstrates why a particular approach is flawed; the second describes a way to amend that approach.	*No, the first supports the alternate strategy—it doesn't illustrate a flaw. I don't even need to read the second half of this choice.*	D̶
(E) The first is a factor used to rationalize a particular strategy; the second is a factor against that strategy.	*Something used to "rationalize" a "strategy"? Yes, that could be describing a premise that supports the alternate strategy. Oh, but the second goes against the strategy? No! The second is actually the author's strategy.*	E

A̶ Ⓑ C̶ D̶ E̶

7. Gray Wolf Population: The correct answer is **(A)**.

Step 1: Identify the question.

The environmentalist challenges the government representative's argument by doing which of the following?	*There's a 2-person-talking structure, and I'm asked how the second person responds; this is a Describe the Argument question.*	DA A B C D E

Step 2: Deconstruct the argument.

Government representative: Between 1996 and 2005, the gray wolf population in Minnesota grew nearly 50%; the gray wolf population in Montana increased by only 13% during the same period.	*This is just a straight fact. The Minnesota wolf population grew a lot faster in that time period than the Montana wolf population.*	Gov rep: 96-05, wolf in Minn ↑ 50%, in Mont only ↑ 13%
Clearly, the Minnesota gray wolf population is more likely to survive and thrive long term.	*Conclusion! Claiming that Minnesota wolves are more likely to survive and thrive. Certainly, the Minnesota wolf population grew more…but does that automatically mean they're more likely to survive and thrive?*	©Minn > likely to survive/ thrive
Environmentalist: But the gray wolf population in Montana is nearly 8 times the population in Minnesota; above a certain critical breeding number, the population is stable and does not require growth in order to survive.	*Ah, okay. The environmentalist is pointing out that they're not necessarily the same thing. Once the population is large enough, it's already stable, so growth isn't necessarily critical to survival.*	Enviro: BUT Mont 8x Minn; when ↑ enough, pop = stable

3

Step 3: State the goal.

The gov rep concludes that the Minnesota wolves are more likely to survive and thrive because the growth rate was a lot higher, but the environmentalist responded that the Montana population was already a lot larger, so growth might not have been necessary to keep the population thriving. The Montana population might already have been stable in the first place.

I need to find something that explains this response in a more abstract way: a new piece of evidence changes the way someone would think about the issue addressed in the conclusion (surviving and thriving).

Step 4: Work from wrong to right.

(A) introducing additional evidence that undermines an assumption made by the representative	*This sounds pretty good. The environmentalist's statement is a new piece of evidence, and it does undermine the government rep's assumption that growth is a good indicator of likelihood to survive and thrive.*	A̰
(B) challenging the representative's definition of a critical breeding number	*The environmentalist challenges the rep's assumption about what it takes to survive and thrive, but the environmentalist can't challenge the rep on "critical breeding number," because the rep never mentions this concept.*	B̶
(C) demonstrating that the critical breeding number of the two wolf populations differs significantly	*The environmentalist mentions the concept of "critical breeding number," but establishes only that the number of wolves in each population differs significantly, not that the number of wolves needed to achieve the "critical breeding number" is different.*	C̶
(D) implying that the two populations of wolves could be combined in order to preserve the species	*This might be an interesting strategy, but the environmentalist never mentions it.*	D̶
(E) suggesting that the Montana wolf population grew at a faster rate than stated in the representative's argument	*This is tricky. The environmentalist introduces a new figure, but that figure has to do with the size of the two populations, not the rate of growth. The environmentalist does not dispute the rep's figures for rate of growth.*	E

Ⓐ　B̶　C̶　D̶　E̶

Chapter 4 of Critical Reasoning

The Assumption Family: Find the Assumption

In This Chapter...

Assumption Family Questions

Find the Assumption (FA) Questions

The Negation Technique

Chapter 4
The Assumption Family: Find the Assumption

Assumptions were introduced briefly in Chapter 2, but did not play a role in Structure Family questions. They are the key to the largest family of questions, the Assumption Family; all five question types in this family contain arguments that involve at least one assumption made by the author. (The "author," refers to the hypothetical person who is "arguing" the argument and believes that argument to be valid. "The author" does not refer to the test writer.)

An assumption is something that *the author must believe to be true* in order to draw a certain conclusion; however, the author *does not state* the assumption in the argument. The assumption itself might not necessarily be true in the real world; rather, the *author* believes that it is true in order to make his or her argument.

For example, what does the author of the below argument assume must be true?

> No athletes under the age of 14 can qualify for Country Y's Olympic team. Therefore, Adrienne can't qualify for Country Y's Olympic team.

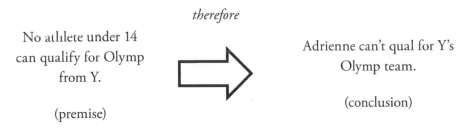

No athlete under 14
can qualify for Olymp
from Y.

(premise)

therefore

Adrienne can't qual for Y's
Olymp team.

(conclusion)

The author assumes that this premise applies to Adrienne—in other words, that she is an athlete from Country Y, and that she is under the age of 14. There may be other reasons she would not qualify for the Olympic team (perhaps her sport is not included), but if she can't qualify *for this reason*, then it must be because she is otherwise qualified (that is, she is an athlete from Country Y) but is too young.

The diagram above represents the **core** of the argument, as discussed in Chapter 1. The core consists of the conclusion and the main premise or premises that lead to that conclusion, as well as the unstated *assumption(s)*. You need assumptions as much as you need any other piece of the argument to make the whole thing work. After all, if Adrienne were *not* under 14, then the argument above would make no sense.

Assumptions fill at least part of a gap in the argument; the gap is represented by the arrow in the diagram above. If you insert a valid assumption into the argument, it makes the argument much better:

> No athletes under the age of 14 can qualify for Country Y's Olympic team. *Adrienne is an athlete from Country Y who is under the age of 14.* Therefore, Adrienne can't compete for Country Y's Olympic team.

therefore

No athlete under 14 can qualify for Olymp from Y.

(premise)

⇒

Adrienne can't qual for Y's Olymp team.

(conclusion)

Adrienne is an athlete from Country Y who is under the age of 14.

(assumption)

The argument above has a single obvious assumption that fills the gap on its own. Most GMAT arguments contain multiple assumptions, none of which individually fill the gap. Any one assumption will not automatically make the argument airtight, but it will make the argument more likely to be true, and the argument will depend on each of those assumptions. Take any assumption away, and the argument collapses.

In order to train yourself to notice the presence of assumptions, think of the person in your life with whom you argue or disagree the most. Whenever you talk to him or her, your brain is already on the offensive. "Really? I'm not so sure about that. You've failed to consider …" Pretend this person is the one making the argument to you. How would you try to pick it apart? You'll be attacking assumptions.

Okay, are you ready? Brainstorm some assumptions for the following argument:

> Thomas's football team lost in the championship game last year. The same two teams are playing in the championship game again this year, and the players on Thomas's team have improved. Therefore, Thomas's team will win the championship game this year.

Picture that person with whom you argue; what would you say? "You're just *assuming* that Thomas's team has improved enough to be competitive with last year's winning team! You're also assuming that last year's winning team has *not* improved enough to keep themselves clearly ahead of Thomas's team!" As you brainstorm, however, remember that on the GMAT, you never have to come up with any assumption in a vacuum. After all, the test is multiple-choice! If you are asked to find an assumption, one of the choices will be a valid assumption, and the other four choices will not be. So, while it's worth reading critically to poke holes in weak arguments, don't spend too much time thinking up assumptions on your own.

Here are a couple of important strategies for dealing with assumptions on the test:

Do		Don't
Notice gaps and articulate assumptions you can think of relatively easily.	**but**	Don't spend more than about 20 seconds brainstorming up front.
Look for your brainstormed assumptions in the answers.	**but**	Don't eliminate answers just because they don't match any of your brainstormed assumptions.
Choose an answer that the author must believe to be true in order to draw the conclusion.	**but**	Don't hold out for something that makes the conclusion "perfect" or definitely true.

Try inserting a brainstormed assumption into the football argument to see how it works:

> Thomas's football team lost in the championship game last year. The same two teams are playing in the championship game again this year, and the players on Thomas's team have improved enough to be competitive with the defending champion team. Therefore, Thomas's team will win the championship game this year.

If the author is going to claim that the improvement will lead to a victory for Thomas's team, then it is *necessary* for the author to believe that this improvement was enough to put that team at least at the same level as the defending champion team. Otherwise, it wouldn't make sense to say that, because these players have improved, they will win this year.

It is still not a foregone conclusion that Thomas's team will definitely win, even though the author clearly believes so. There are too many other potential factors involved; the author is making many assumptions, not just one. It is only necessary to find one assumption, though; it is not necessary to make the argument foolproof.

Drill: Brainstorm Assumptions

Brainstorm at least one assumption that must be true in order to make each argument. If you like, you can draw out the argument core.

1. Sculptors do not work in a practical field. Therefore, Charles does not work in a practical field.

2. The employees of Quick Corp's accounting department consistently show a significant jump in productivity in the two weeks before taking vacation. Clearly, the knowledge that they are about to go on vacation motivates the employees to be more productive.

3. Mayor: The Acme Factory has developed a new manufacturing process that uses chemical Q, the residue of which is toxic to babies. In order to protect our children, we need to pass a law banning the use of this chemical.

Answer Key for Drill: Brainstorm Assumptions

Possible assumptions are noted in italics below the arrow. You may brainstorm different assumptions from the ones shown. Other assumptions are acceptable as long as they represent something that MUST be true in order to make the given argument.

1.

Sculptors do NOT work in practical field.

therefore

C does NOT work in practical field.

Charles is a sculptor.

The author is arguing that this premise applies to Charles—in other words, he must be a sculptor.

2.

2 wks b4 vaca:
↑ prod

therefore

emp choose >>
prod b4 vaca

They didn't plan vacation to occur right after a big deadline or other busy time.

The author concludes that employees decide to be more productive *because* they'll be taking vacation soon. Perhaps it's the case, instead, that the employees choose to take vacation right after they know they'll be *forced* to work harder for some other reason. For example, maybe everyone in the accounting department takes vacation right after the annual financial report is due. The author is assuming that *other* causes of the jump in productivity don't apply in this case.

3.

Acme using Q, toxic baby

therefore

to protect kids, ban Q

If Acme uses Q, then kids will somehow come into contact with Q.

The author assumes that use of chemical Q in the production process will somehow eventually expose babies to the chemical residue. Maybe the chemical is used only for something that never comes into contact with the final product and will never come into contact with kids.

MANHATTAN
PREP

Assumption Family Questions

There are five types of assumption questions. The first major type, Find the Assumption, is covered in this chapter. In Chapter 5, you'll learn about the next two major types: Strengthen the Argument and Weaken the Argument. Chapter 6 covers the two remaining types in the Assumption Family: Evaluate the Argument and Find the Flaw.

Each type of question has its own key characteristics and goals, but some characteristics are common to all five types. There will always be a conclusion, so you definitely want to look for it. In addition, *while you read*, you should try to notice any gaps, indicating assumptions, that jump out at you (but don't take much longer than you normally take to read the argument itself).

Find the Assumption (FA) Questions

Find the Assumption questions ask you to, well, find an assumption that the author must believe to be true in order to make the argument. The correct answer should make the argument possible. If the correct answer were *not* true, the argument would not be valid.

Your task is to figure out which answer choice represents something that must hold true according to the author. Note one especially tricky aspect of these problems: the assumption itself might only be true in the mind of the author. You might think, "Well, is that really true in the real world? I don't think that has to be true." Don't ask that question! The only issue is whether the *author* must believe it to be true in order to arrive at his or her conclusion. If the argument is "Planets are wonderful; therefore, Pluto is wonderful," then the assumption is that Pluto is a planet (whether you still think it is or not).

Identifying the Question

These questions are usually easy to identify, because the question stem will use some form of the noun "assumption" or the verb "to assume." Occasionally, the question may ask for a new premise, or a new piece of information, that is "required" or a new premise that will help the conclusion to be "more reasonably drawn" (or similar language). Here are a couple of examples:

> Which of the following is an *assumption* on which the argument depends?

> The *conclusion above* would be *more reasonably drawn* if it were established that

Try this sample argument:

> When news periodicals begin forecasting a recession, people tend to spend less money on nonessential purchases. Therefore, the perceived threat of a future recession decreases the willingness of people to purchase products that they regard as optional or luxury goods.
>
> Which of the following is an assumption on which the argument depends?

Do the first couple of steps before looking at the answer choices:

Step 1: Identify the question.

Which of the following is an assumption on which the argument depends?	*The question stem uses the word "assumption," so it is the Assumption type. Write "FA" on the scrap paper and then the answer choice letters.*	FA A B C D E

Step 2: Deconstruct the argument.

When news periodicals begin forecasting a recession, people tend to spend less money on nonessential purchases.	*This sounds like a premise, though I suppose it could be a conclusion. The news periodicals predict a recession, and then people spend less money.*	Periodicals forecast recess → ppl spend ↓ $ non-ess
Therefore, the perceived threat of a future recession decreases the willingness of people to purchase products that they regard as optional or luxury goods.	*This is the conclusion. The premise above tells what people do—spend less money. The conclusion tries to claim <u>why</u> they do it—a perceived future threat.*	Ⓒ Perceived threat → ppl spend ↓ $ lux
	What is the author assuming? That people are actually reading or hearing about the forecasts. That the recession hasn't already started and <u>that's</u> why people are spending less money— maybe the periodicals are just slow in "forecasting" something that has already started. Also, the author assumes that "nonessential" and "luxury" mean the same thing.	

Did you come up with any other assumptions? The key is to get your brain thinking about these things, but there are almost always multiple possible assumptions; you may not brainstorm the exact one that will show up in the answers.

Step 3: State the goal.

Articulate the core to yourself. You don't necessarily need to write/draw it out unless you want to.

therefore

Periodicals forecast:
recess! ↓ spend non-ess

Perceived threat → spend
lux $ ↓

People reading/hearing info
from periodicals.
Threat only perceived today;
recession hasn't already started.

Look for the assumptions you brainstormed but also be flexible; you might not have thought of the assumption in the correct answer or the assumption you thought of may be phrased differently than you imagined. On FA questions, traps often involve an answer that is not tied to the conclusion, an answer that makes the argument weaker, not stronger, or an answer that makes an irrelevant distinction or comparison. (Note: you'll learn more about trap answers later in the chapter.)

Take a look at the full problem now:

> When news periodicals begin forecasting a recession, people tend to spend less money on nonessential purchases. Therefore, the perceived threat of a future recession decreases the willingness of people to purchase products that they regard as optional or luxury goods.
>
> Which of the following is an assumption on which the argument depends?
>
> (A) People do not always agree as to which goods should be considered luxury goods.
> (B) Many more people read news periodicals today than five years ago.
> (C) Most people do not regularly read news periodicals.
> (D) Decreased spending on nonessential goods does not prompt news periodicals to forecast a recession.
> (E) At least some of the biggest spending consumers prior to the recession were among those who curtailed their spending after the recession began.

Step 4: Work from wrong to right.

(A) People do not always agree as to which goods should be considered luxury goods.	*I can believe that this is true in the real world, but this is irrelevant to the conclusion. The argument is not based upon whether people agree as to how to classify certain goods.*	~~A~~
(B) Many more people read news periodicals today than five years ago.	*This sounds a little bit like one of my brainstormed assumptions—the argument assumes that people are actually reading those periodicals. I'm not so sure about the "more today than five years ago" part, though. You don't absolutely have to believe that in order to draw that conclusion. I'll keep it in for now, but maybe I'll find something better.*	B
(C) Most people do not regularly read news periodicals.	*This is also about reading the periodicals...but it's the opposite of what I want! The argument needs to assume that people DO read the periodicals; if they don't, then how can they be influenced by what the periodicals forecast?*	~~C~~
(D) Decreased spending on nonessential goods does not prompt news periodicals to forecast a recession.	*Let's see. This choice is saying that the drop in spending is not <u>itself</u> causing the forecasts. That's good, because the argument is that the causality runs the other way: the forecasts cause the drop in spending. This one is looking better than answer (B). I can cross off (B) now.*	~~B~~ D
(E) At least some of the biggest spending consumers prior to the recession were among those who curtailed their spending after the recession began.	*Hmm. This one sounds good, too. Maybe if the biggest spenders keep spending during the recession, then the overall amount of money being spent won't go down that much...although the argument doesn't really seem to depend on how much it goes down. Oh, wait: this says "<u>after</u> the recession began"—but the conclusion is about a "perceived threat of a <u>future</u> recession." Nice trap!*	~~E~~

        ~~A~~   ~~B~~   ~~C~~   ⓓ   ~~E~~

There were a couple of good brainstormed assumptions, but none that matched the exact assumption contained in the correct answer, (**D**). That's okay; be prepared to be flexible!

Note that answer choice (C) contained an "opposite" answer: it weakened the conclusion rather than making it stronger.

The Negation Technique

On harder questions, you might find yourself stuck between two answer choices. To unstick yourself, try the Negation technique.

On Find the Assumption questions, the correct answer will be something that the author must believe to be true in order to make his or her argument. As a result, if you were to turn the correct answer around to make the opposite point, then the author's argument should be harmed. Negating the correct answer should weaken the author's conclusion.

Try it out on the News Periodicals problem from above. Say that you narrowed the answers to (B) and (D):

> (B)   Many more people read news periodicals today than five years ago.
>
> (D)   Decreased spending on nonessential goods does not prompt news periodicals to forecast a recession.

Recall the argument itself as mapped out above:

> Periodicals forecast recess → ppl spend ↓ $ non-ess
>
> Perceived threat → ppl spend ↓ $ lux

The author argues that when the periodicals forecast a recession, people perceive a future threat, and so people choose to spend less money on luxury goods.

What if answer choice (B) was NOT true? It would say something like:

> (B)   The same number or fewer people read news periodicals today than five years ago.

Does this weaken the author's conclusion? Not really. While the argument does assume that at least some people are reading news periodicals, it doesn't discuss what used to happen five years ago, nor does it hinge on any sort of change over time.

Try negating answer (D):

> (D)   Decreased spending on nonessential goods DOES prompt news periodicals to forecast a recession.

Hmm. If spending goes down and then the news periodicals react by forecasting a recession…then the author has it backwards! The news periodicals aren't causing a behavior change in consumers. Rather, they're reacting to something the consumers are already doing. Thus, the argument no longer works. Negating this answer breaks down the author's argument, so this choice is the right answer.

A word of warning: don't use this technique on every answer choice or you'll be in danger of spending too much time. However, when you're stuck, the Negation technique can be a big help. And if *that* doesn't work, as always, you know what to do: guess and move on.

Common Trap Answers

On many Find the Assumption questions, a trap answer won't actually address the conclusion. Because the question specifically asks you to find an assumption necessary to draw that conclusion, an answer that has **No Tie to the Conclusion** must be wrong. Answer (A) in the problem above is a good example. The conclusion does not depend upon whether different people would agree to classify the same item as a luxury good. Rather, the conclusion is about what causes someone to spend less money on anything that that individual believes to be a luxury good.

Trap answers can also use **Reverse Logic**, as in answer choice (C). Reverse logic does the opposite of what you want; in this case, answer (C) actually makes the argument worse, but an assumption should make the argument a bit stronger.

Answers (B) and (E) are examples of another trap: making an **Irrelevant Distinction or Comparison**. The argument does not hinge upon whether people read more now than they did five years ago. Nor does it depend upon the highest spending consumers doing something different from the rest of consumers. Rather, all consumers are lumped together in the argument.

Cheat Sheet

Find the Assumption Cheat Sheet

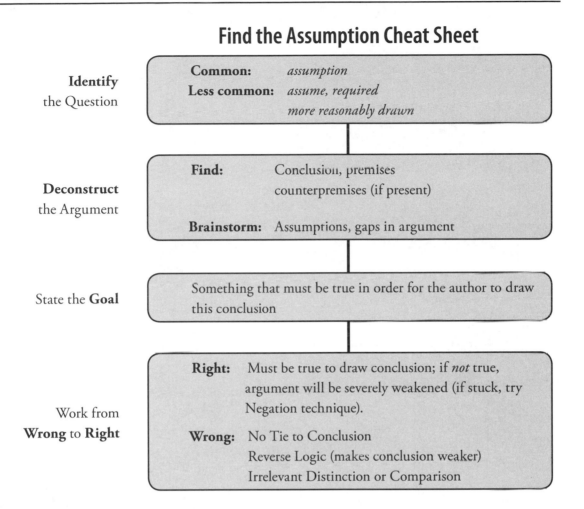

Identify the Question

> **Common:**   *assumption*
> **Less common:**   *assume, required*
>   *more reasonably drawn*

Deconstruct the Argument

> **Find:**   Conclusion, premises
>   counterpremises (if present)
>
> **Brainstorm:** Assumptions, gaps in argument

State the **Goal**

> Something that must be true in order for the author to draw this conclusion

Work from **Wrong** to **Right**

> **Right:**   Must be true to draw conclusion; if *not* true, argument will be severely weakened (if stuck, try Negation technique).
>
> **Wrong:**   No Tie to Conclusion
>   Reverse Logic (makes conclusion weaker)
>   Irrelevant Distinction or Comparison

4

Photocopy this page and keep it with the review sheets you're creating as you study. Better yet, use this page as a guide to create your own review sheet—you'll remember the material better if you write it down yourself.

Problem Set

Answer each question using the four-step Critical Reasoning process. Check your answer after each question. As you improve, consider timing yourself; CR questions need to be completed in an average of two minutes.

1. *MTC & Asthma*

   Methyltetrachloride (MTC) is a chemical found in some pesticides, glues, and sealants. Exposure to MTC can cause people to develop asthma. In order to halve the nation's asthma rate, the government plans to ban all products containing MTC.

   The government's plan to halve the nation's asthma rate relies on which of the following assumptions?

   (A) Exposure to MTC is responsible for no less than half of the nation's asthma cases.
   (B) Products containing MTC are not necessary to the prosperity of the American economy.
   (C) Asthma has reached epidemic proportions.
   (D) Exercise and proper nutrition are helpful in maintaining respiratory health.
   (E) Dust mites and pet dander can also cause asthma.

2. *Oil and Ethanol*

   Country N's oil production is not sufficient to meet its domestic demand. In order to sharply reduce its dependence on foreign sources of oil, Country N recently embarked on a program requiring all of its automobiles to run on ethanol in addition to gasoline. Combined with its oil production, Country N produces enough ethanol from agricultural by-products to meet its current demand for energy.

   Which of the following must be assumed in order to conclude that Country N will succeed in its plan to reduce its dependence on foreign oil?

   (A) Electric power is not a superior alternative to ethanol in supplementing automobile gasoline consumption.
   (B) In Country N, domestic production of ethanol is increasing more quickly than domestic oil production.
   (C) Ethanol is suitable for the heating of homes and other applications aside from automobiles.
   (D) In Country N, gasoline consumption is not increasing at a substantially higher rate than domestic oil and ethanol production.
   (E) Ethanol is as efficient as gasoline in terms of mileage per gallon when used as fuel for automobiles.

3. *Exchange Student*

Student Advisor: One of our exchange students faced multiple arguments with her parents over the course of the past year. Not surprisingly, her grade point average (GPA) over the same period showed a steep decline. This is just one example of a general truth: problematic family relationships can cause significant academic difficulties for our students.\

Which of the following is required for the Student Advisor to claim that problematic family relationships can cause academic difficulties?

(A) Last year, the exchange student reduced the amount of time spent on academic work, resulting in a lower GPA.

(B) The decline in the GPA of the exchange student was not the reason for the student's arguments with her parents.

(C) School GPA is an accurate measure of a student's intellectual ability.

(D) If proper measures are not taken, the decline in the student's academic performance may become irreversible.

(E) Fluctuations in academic performance are typical for many students.

4. *News War*

For several years, Nighttime News attracted fewer viewers than World News, which broadcasts its show at the same time as Nighttime News. Recently, the producers of Nighttime News added personal interest stories and increased coverage of sports and weather. The two programs now have a roughly equal number of viewers. Clearly, the recent programming changes persuaded viewers to switch from World News to Nighttime News.

The conclusion above is properly drawn if which of the following is assumed?

(A) Viewers are more interested in sports and weather than in personal interest stories.

(B) The programming content of Nighttime News is more closely aligned with the interests of the overall audience than is the content of World News.

(C) Some World News viewers liked the new Nighttime News programming better than they liked the World News programming.

(D) There are other possible causes for an increase in the number of viewers of Nighttime News, including a recent ad campaign that aired on many local affiliates.

(E) The quality of World News will remain constant even if Nighttime News improves.

5. *Genetics*

Two genes, BRCA1 and BRCA2, are linked to hereditary breast cancer. Therefore, in order to decrease the annual number of mammogram tests administered across a population and to more accurately assess a woman's individual risk of breast cancer, all women should be tested for these genes.

Which of the following is an assumption on which the argument depends?

(A) Some of the women who are tested for the two genes will subsequently undergo mammograms on a less frequent basis than they used to.

(B) The majority of breast cancer patients have no family history of the disease.

(C) Researchers may have identified a third breast cancer gene that is linked with hereditary breast cancer.

(D) Women who have these genes have an 80% chance of getting breast cancer, while women who do not have these genes have only a 10% chance of getting breast cancer.

(E) The presence of BRCA1 and BRCA2 can explain up to 50% of hereditary cases.

4

Solutions

1. MTC & Asthma: The correct answer is **(A)**.

Step 1: Identify the question.

The government's plan to halve the nation's asthma rate relies on which of the following assumptions?	*Asks for the "assumption"; this is a Find the Assumption question.*	FA A B C D E

Step 2: Deconstruct the argument

Methyltetrachloride (MTC) is a chemical found in some pesticides, glues, and sealants.	*This is just a fact—background or maybe a premise.*	MTC = chem
Exposure to MTC can cause people to develop asthma.	*Another fact but it's specifically a bad fact. This is likely a premise.*	can → asthma
In order to halve the nation's asthma rate, the government plans to ban all products containing MTC.	*Okay, the government has a plan to ban MTC, and the result will be (they claim) that the asthma rate will be cut in half. There are no numbers or anything to support that. Are a lot of people exposed now? What percentage of those who develop asthma were exposed? Etc.*	©gov plan: ban MTC to ½ asthma rate

Step 3: State the goal.

The government claims that it can halve the asthma rate by banning MTC, but it gives absolutely no evidence or numbers to support <u>halving</u> the rate.

I need to find an answer that supports the idea that they can halve the asthma rate—maybe that a very large percentage of people who develop asthma were exposed to MTC or something like that.

Step 4: Work from wrong to right.

(A) Exposure to MTC is responsible for no less than half of the nation's asthma cases.	*This sounds similar to what I said. Let's see. If MTC actually is responsible for at least half of asthma cases, then getting rid of it would get rid of all those cases as well. This one looks pretty good.*	A̰
(B) Products containing MTC are not necessary to the prosperity of the American economy.	*Prosperity of the economy? They're just trying to distract me by making me think of a reason why we might be able to ban MTC without adverse consequences. The conclusion is about halving the asthma rate, and this doesn't affect that conclusion.*	B̶
(C) Asthma has reached epidemic proportions.	*If asthma rates are really high, then that supports the idea of wanting to lower them. But that's not what I'm trying to find—the author doesn't have to believe that there's an epidemic of asthma. Plus it says nothing about whether MTC is the cause.*	C̶
(D) Exercise and proper nutrition are helpful in maintaining respiratory health.	*Distraction! Nothing about how or whether MTC causes asthma, or whether getting rid of MTC will lower asthma rates.*	D̶
(E) Dust mites and pet dander can also cause asthma.	*Distraction! Nothing about how or whether MTC causes asthma, or whether getting rid of MTC will lower asthma rates.*	E̶

Ⓐ   B̶   C̶   D̶   E̶

2. Oil and Ethanol: The correct answer is (**D**).

Step 1: Identify the question.

Which of the following must be assumed in order to conclude that Country N will succeed in its plan to reduce its dependence on foreign oil?	*Contains the phrase "must be assumed"—this is a Find the Assumption question.*	FA A B C D E

Step 2: Deconstruct the argument.

Country N's oil production is not sufficient to meet its domestic demand.	*They produce oil but can't make enough for their own needs. That must mean they have to import some oil.*	N oil prod < dom demand
In order to sharply reduce its dependence on foreign sources of oil, Country N recently embarked on a program requiring all of its automobiles to run on ethanol in addition to gasoline.	*They're requiring cars to use ethanol, and they think that'll lead to having to use less foreign oil. It sounds like the cars can still use gas, though…*	To ↓ for. oil, N reqs ethanol in cars
Combined with its oil production, Country N produces enough ethanol from agricultural by-products to meet its current demand for energy.	*Okay, so they do make enough ethanol PLUS oil combined to satisfy their own needs currently. The question is whether people are actually going to use ethanol for their cars or whether they'll want to keep using gasoline. And what if demand changes in future?*	N eth + oil = curr demand

Step 3: State the goal.

Country N thinks it can "sharply reduce" the amount of foreign oil it needs if it starts making people own cars that use ethanol. Will the plan really work that way? They're assuming people really will start to use the ethanol. They're also assuming they'll continue to produce enough oil and ethanol in the future.

I need to find an answer that must be true in order to allow the author to draw the above conclusion.

Step 4: Work from wrong to right.

(A) Electric power is not a superior alternative to ethanol in supplementing automobile gasoline consumption.	*Electric power? That seems out of scope. We're supposed to find something that goes with the plan stated in the argument, and that plan mentions nothing about electric power.*	A̶
(B) In Country N, domestic production of ethanol is increasing more quickly than domestic oil production.	*If this is true, then switching stuff to ethanol seems like a good call. Does it have to be true in order to draw the conclusion? What if the two were increasing at the same rate? That would be fine, actually. This doesn't have to be true—so it isn't a necessary assumption.*	B̶
(C) Ethanol is suitable for the heating of homes and other applications aside from automobiles.	*If this is true, then switching stuff to ethanol seems like a good call. Does it have to be true in order to draw the conclusion? No. The argument only talks about a plan to have cars start using ethanol.*	C̶
(D) In Country N, gasoline consumption is not increasing at a substantially higher rate than domestic oil and ethanol production.	*Hmm. The argument is assuming in general that the ethanol + oil production can keep up with the country's demand. So, yes, the author would have to assume that gas consumption isn't increasing at a much faster rate than production.* *Let's try negating this one: If gas consumption were increasing at a much higher rate, what would happen? Oh, they might have to get more from foreign sources—bingo! Negating this does weaken the conclusion.*	D̰
(E) Ethanol is as efficient as gasoline in terms of mileage per gallon when used as fuel for automobiles.	*It would be good to know how efficient ethanol is compared to gas…but does it <u>have</u> to be true that they're <u>equally</u> efficient? No. Even if ethanol were less efficient, it's possible that the country could still produce enough to meet its needs.*	E̶

A̶   B̶   C̶   Ⓓ   E̶

3. Exchange Student: The correct answer is **(B)**.

Step 1: Identify the question.

Which of the following is required for the Student Advisor to claim that problematic family relationships can cause academic difficulties?	*This is an unusual question stem. It doesn't include the word "assumption" but it does include a synonymous idea: what is __required__ to draw the conclusion? This is an assumption question.*	FA A B C D E

Step 2: Deconstruct the argument.

Student Advisor: One of our exchange students faced multiple arguments with her parents over the course of the past year.	*This is a fact—background or a premise.*	Advisor: student had args w parents
Not surprisingly, her grade point average (GPA) over the same period showed a steep decline.	*Not only did the student's GPA go down, but the advisor says "not surprisingly." Sounds like the advisor is going to conclude a causal relationship.*	GPA ↓↓
This is just one example of a general truth: problematic family relationships can cause significant academic difficulties for our students.	*Here we go: the advisor claims that this student's family problems __caused__ the academic problems. Maybe there was a different cause.*	↓ ⓒ fam probs → acad probs

Step 3: State the goal.

I need to find an answer that the author must believe to be true in order to draw this conclusion. The only thing I can think of right now is very general: if the advisor is assuming the family problems were what caused the academic problems, then the advisor is also assuming there wasn't something else causing the academic problems.

Step 4: Work from wrong to right.

(A) Last year, the exchange student reduced the amount of time spent on academic work, resulting in a lower GPA.	*This would explain why her GPA went down, which means maybe it didn't actually have to do with family problems. But I'm looking for something the author believes will help with the claim that it was family problems. This answer hurts that claim.*	~~A~~
(B) The decline in the GPA of the exchange student was not the reason for the student's arguments with her parents.	*Let's see. This is kind of what I said before—there is not a different cause for the decline of her GPA.* *Let's try negating this. If the student's GPA went down first and then her parents got mad at her for that reason, then you can't claim that the family problems caused the lower GPA. The advisor's argument would fall apart. This choice looks good.*	B̰
(C) School GPA is an accurate measure of a student's intellectual ability.	*This point doesn't matter. Either the measure is accurate or it's inaccurate. Regardless, this student's GPA used to be higher and is now lower, and she and her parents have been arguing about something. Whether her GPA is an accurate measure of her ability doesn't come into consideration in the argument.*	~~C~~
(D) If proper measures are not taken, the decline in the student's academic performance may become irreversible.	*I could see how this point might be plausible in general, but it isn't necessary for the claim that family problems can cause academic problems. Therefore, it can't possibly be the assumption.*	~~D~~
(E) Fluctuations in academic performance are typical for many students.	*Like choice (D), this choice may be plausible, but it isn't necessary for the conclusion, so it can't possibly be the assumption.*	E

~~A~~   Ⓑ   ~~C~~   ~~D~~   ~~E~~

4. News War: The correct answer is **(C)**.

Step 1: Identify the question.

The conclusion above is properly drawn if which of the following is assumed?	*The word "assumed" tells me that this is a Find the Assumption question.*	FA A B C D E

Step 2: Deconstruct the argument.

For several years, Nighttime News attracted fewer viewers than World News, which broadcasts its show at the same time as Nighttime News.	*NNews and WNews are competitors. In the past, WNews got more viewers. Facts = premises.*	Past: NNews < WNews
Recently, the producers of Nighttime News added personal interest stories and increased coverage of sports and weather.	*NNews added certain new things.*	Recent: NNews added + pers, spports, weath
The two programs now have a roughly equal number of viewers.	*Now, the two audiences are about equal in number. Interesting. Why? So far, all premises.*	Now: same #
Clearly, the recent programming changes persuaded viewers to switch from World News to Nighttime News.	*Conclusion! The author is claiming Ⓒ that the new programming actually caused people to <u>switch</u> from one show to the other. Hmm—that would mean WNews's numbers went down—did they? Or is it just that NNews went up? Or maybe there's some other reason for the change entirely.*	prog Δ → switch

Step 3: State the goal.

The author is claiming specifically that people <u>switched</u> from WNews to NNews—but there's no evidence for that. The author is assuming that, if NNews's numbers went up, then WNews's numbers went down and that those people switched to NNews (and didn't start watching something else or turn off their TVs entirely!).

The author's also assuming that the reason for the switch was NNews's new programming and not something else.

I need to find an answer that represents something the author must believe to be true.

Step 4: Work from wrong to right.

(A) Viewers are more interested in sports and weather than in personal interest stories.	*Hmm. NNews added all three of these things. Does the author need to assume that two are more popular than the third? No—it doesn't matter as long as the programming in general did make people switch. Maybe they're trying to get me to think that the choice is comparing WNews and NNews—but that's not what this choice actually says.*	A̶
(B) The programming content of Nighttime News is more closely aligned with the interests of the overall audience than is the content of World News.	*This basically says that the audience likes NNews's content better than WNews's content. That could be a reason to switch. Does it absolutely have to be true? It also addresses the programming issue, so it does seem pretty good—I'll leave it in for now.*	B̰
(C) Some World News viewers liked the new Nighttime News programming better than they liked the World News programming.	*This also talks about liking NNews better than WNews. In particular, it says that some WNews viewers decided they liked the new NNews stuff better. That also looks really good. Leave it in.*	C̰
(D) There are other possible causes for an increase in the number of viewers of Nighttime News, including a recent ad campaign that aired on many local affiliates.	*"Other possible causes"—oh, no, are all three of these choices good? Wait a second. I'm reading this backwards. This is saying there are other reasons why more people are watching NNews, so that would actually hurt the author's claim that it's because WNews viewers switched due to the programming.*	D̶
(E) The quality of World News will remain constant even if Nighttime News improves.	*If this were true, it might help explain why some people would switch, but does it <u>have</u> to be true in order to claim that people already switched due to NNews's new programming? No.*	E̶
Compare (B) and (C)	*Hmm. I'll try negating (B) and (C).* *(B): NNews content is not more closely aligned with audience than WNews content. Maybe they're about the same? That doesn't really hurt the author's argument all that much.* *(C): None of the WNews viewers liked NNews better than WNews. Wait a second. If <u>none</u> of them liked NNews better, why would they switch? Negating this definitely hurts the argument. So Choice (C) must be necessary. Choice (C) it is!*	B̰ Ⓒ

A̶　　B̰　　Ⓒ　　D̶　　E̶

MANHATTAN
PREP

5. Genetics: The correct answer is (A).

Step 1: Identify the question.

Which of the following is an assumption on which the argument depends?	*The word "assumption" indicates that this is a Find the Assumption question.*	FA A B C D E

Step 2: Deconstruct the argument.

Two genes, BRCA1 and BRCA2, are linked to hereditary breast cancer.	*Straight fact.*	2 genes linked to b-cancer
Therefore, in order to decrease the annual number of mammogram tests administered across a population and to more accurately assess a woman's individual risk of breast cancer, all women should be tested for these genes.	*Complicated. Okay, the author's recommending that all women be tested and claims this will do two things: decrease the # of mammograms and better assess risk. So one assumption could be that those who test negatively won't get a mammogram as frequently.*	©To ↓ mammos + assess risk, should test all women

Step 3: State the goal.

The author claims that, if women are all tested for these genes, two things will happen: the number of mammograms will go down __and__ they'll be able to assess risk more accurately.

I need to find an answer that the author must believe to be true in drawing this conclusion. That might have something to do with the number of mammograms or with assessing risk.

Step 4: Work from wrong to right

(A) Some of the women who are tested for the two genes will subsequently undergo mammograms on a less frequent basis than they used to.	*If at least some women get tested and then get fewer mammograms, then that would help to reduce the number of mammograms. But does this have to be true? Actually, I think so. It has to be the case that women who otherwise would have gotten mammograms don't; otherwise, the number can't go down.*	A
(B) The majority of breast cancer patients have no family history of the disease.	*I'm not sure how this affects the "number of mammograms" claim, but I think it actually hurts the "better assess risk" claim. It seems like the argument assumes that if you don't have the gene, you won't get mammograms, but then this choice says a lot of women who do get breast cancer don't have a family history. Also, someone can have a gene and not develop breast cancer, so maybe that's why there's no family history. Too many "ifs" on this one.*	B
(C) Researchers may have identified a third breast cancer gene that is linked with hereditary breast cancer.	*If so, then presumably the author of the argument might want to add this third one to the list. But that has nothing to do with the argument as it stands.*	C
(D) Women who have these genes have an 80% chance of getting breast cancer, while women who do not have these genes have only a 10% chance of getting breast cancer.	*If that's true, then it does sound like knowing whether you have the gene would help more accurately assess your risk. Does this have to be true? Not with those specific numbers, actually. Tricky. Maybe it's 70% or 90% instead of 80%; the message is still the same.*	D
(E) The presence of BRCA1 and BRCA2 can explain up to 50% of hereditary cases.	*So, of the women who inherit breast cancer, the genes account for about half of cases. This is kind of like the last one—that specific number doesn't have to be true.*	E

(A)   B   C   D   E

Chapter 5
of
Critical Reasoning

The Assumption Family:
Strengthen and Weaken

In This Chapter...

Strengthen and Weaken: The Basics

Strengthen the Argument Questions

Weaken the Argument Questions

EXCEPT Questions

Chapter 5

The Assumption Family: Strengthen and Weaken

In Chapter 4, you learned about the first major question type in the Assumption Family: Find the Assumption. If you haven't read Chapter 4 yet, please do so before reading this chapter.

To recap briefly:

- Assumptions are something an author must believe to be true in order to draw his or her conclusion. These assumptions are not stated explicitly in the argument.

- All assumption arguments will contain a "core": a conclusion and the major premise or premises that lead to it.

- All assumption arguments will include at least one (and probably more than one) unstated assumption.

This chapter addresses the next two Assumption Family question types: Strengthen the Argument and Weaken the Argument. Like Find the Assumption, these two types are commonly tested on the GMAT. They also hinge upon identifying an assumption.

Strengthen and Weaken: The Basics

Both Strengthen and Weaken questions ask you to find a *new* piece of information that, if added to the existing argument, will make the conclusion either more likely to be true (strengthen) or less likely to be true (weaken).

In the case of a Strengthen, the new piece of information will typically serve as evidence that some assumption is actually valid. In the case of a Weaken, the new piece of info will attack an assumption: it will serve as evidence that the assumption is invalid.

How does this work? Let's look at one of the arguments from the last chapter again:

> Thomas's football team lost in the championship game last year. The same two teams are playing in the championship game again this year, and the players on Thomas's team have improved. Therefore, Thomas's team will win the championship game this year.

If you were asked a Find the Assumption question, the answer might be something like this: Thomas's team has improved enough to be competitive with the defending champions. In order for the author to draw this conclusion, that point must be assumed. If Thomas's team hasn't improved enough to be (at minimum) competitive with last year's first-place team, then it wouldn't make any sense to say that *because* they have improved, they will win this year.

If you're asked a Strengthen question, how does the answer change? A Strengthen answer provides us with some new piece of information that does not have to be true, but *if it is true*, that information does make the conclusion more likely to be valid. For example:

> The star quarterback on the defending champion team will miss the game due to an injury.

Must it be true that the star quarterback will miss the game in order for the author to believe that Thomas's team will win? No. If that information *is* true, though, then the conclusion is more likely to be true. Thomas's team is more likely to win if a star player on the opposing team can't play.

What happens if you're asked a Weaken question? Similarly, a Weaken answer provides a new piece of information that does not have to be true, but *if it is true*, then the conclusion is a bit less likely to be valid. For example:

> The players on the defending champion team train more than the players on any other team.

That specific fact does not have to be true in order for you to doubt the claim that Thomas's team will win—there are lots of reasons to doubt the claim—but *if it is true* that the defending champion team trains more than all of the other teams, then the author's conclusion just got weaker.

Note that Strengthen and Weaken question stems include the words "if true" or an equivalent variation. In other words, you are explicitly told to accept the information in the answer as true.

Finally, there are three possible ways that an answer choice could affect the argument on both Strengthen and Weaken questions: the answer *strengthens* the argument, the answer *weakens* the argument, or the answer *does nothing* to the argument. One of your tasks will be to classify each answer choice into one of these three buckets.

Strengthen the Argument Questions

Strengthen questions ask you to find a *new* piece of information that, if added to the existing argument, will make the argument somewhat more likely to be true.

Most often, Strengthen questions will contain some form of the words "strengthen" or "support," as well as the phrase "if true." Here are some typical examples:

> Which of the following, if true, most strengthens the argument above?

> Which of the following, if true, most strongly supports the mayor's claim?

Strengthen questions will sometimes use synonyms in place of the strengthen/support language including:

- provides the best basis *or* the best reason for
- provides justification for
- provides evidence in favor of (a plan or a conclusion)

Strengthen questions may occasionally lack the exact phrase "if true" but some other wording will provide a similar meaning. That wording might be something quite similar, such as "if feasible" (in reference to a plan). Alternatively, the wording might indicate that the answer can be "effectively achieved" or "successfully accomplished" (indicating that the information would become true).

Try this short example:

> At QuestCorp, many employees have quit recently and taken jobs with a competitor. Shortly before the employees quit, QuestCorp lost its largest client. Clearly, the employees were no longer confident in QuestCorp's long-term viability.
>
> Which of the following, if true, most strengthens the claim that concerns about QuestCorp's viability caused the employees to quit?
>
> (A) Employees at QuestCorp's main competitor recently received a large and well-publicized raise.
>
> (B) QuestCorp's largest client accounted for 40% of sales and nearly 60% of the company's profits.
>
> (C) Many prospective hires who have interviewed with QuestCorp ultimately accepted jobs with other companies.

The question stem indicates that this is a Strengthen question. Deconstruct the argument. The core might be:

therefore

lost client,
ppl quit

quit b/c concern
about success

(premise)

(conclusion)

Remember, you can write the core down or you can just articulate the core to yourself mentally. Whichever path works best for you is fine.

Make sure that you understand what the argument is trying to say. The author claims that, because the company lost its largest client, some employees lost confidence in the company, so they quit. The author assumes that losing that client will be a significant blow to the company. What if the company has many clients and the largest client only represented a very small fraction of the business? The author also assumes there aren't other reasons why employees quit.

Remind yourself of your goal:

> *This is a Strengthen question, so I have to find some evidence that supports the claim that people quit specifically because they lost confidence in the company after it lost its largest client.*

(A) Employees at QuestCorp's main competitor recently received a large and well-publicized raise.	*Wouldn't that make QuestCorp's employees jealous—maybe they'd expect more money? That'd make it more likely that they quit because of $ issues rather than a loss of confidence in the company. If anything, this weakens the conclusion; I want a strengthen answer.*	A̶
(B) QuestCorp's largest client accounted for 40% of sales and nearly 60% of the company's profits.	*Ouch. Then losing this client would be a pretty serious blow to the company. This is a fact that helps make the conclusion a little more likely; I'll keep it in.*	B̰
(C) Many prospective hires who have interviewed with QuestCorp ultimately accepted jobs with other companies.	*Hmm. "Prospective hires" are not employees. I was asked to strengthen the part about <u>employees</u> losing confidence in the company. I could speculate that maybe something is wrong with QuestCorp if people take other jobs … but the answer doesn't even tell me <u>why</u> these people took other jobs. Maybe QuestCorp rejected them!*	C̶

The correct answer is (**B**).

Answer choice (A) represents one common trap on Strengthen questions: the answer does the opposite of what you want. That is, it weakens the conclusion rather than strengthening it.

Answer choice (C) represents another common trap: the answer addresses (and sometimes even strengthens) something other than what you were asked to address. In this case, the answer does seem to imply that there's something not so great about QuestCorp, but it discusses the wrong group of people (prospective hires) and doesn't actually provide any information that allows you to assess what they think of QuestCorp's viability. (Again, that last part doesn't matter in the end, because it's already talking about the wrong group of people in the first place.)

5

Putting It All Together

Try a full problem now:

> Donut Chain, wishing to increase the profitability of its new store, will place a coupon in the local newspaper offering a free donut with a cup of coffee at its grand opening. Donut Chain calculates that the cost of the advertisement and the free donuts will be more than recouped by the new business generated through the promotion.
>
> Which of the following, if true, most strengthens the prediction that Donut Chain's promotion will increase the new store's profitability?
>
> (A) Donut Chain has a loyal following in much of the country.
> (B) Donut Chain has found that the vast majority of new visitors to its stores become regular customers.
> (C) One donut at Donut Chain costs less than a cup of coffee.
> (D) Most of the copies of the coupon in the local newspaper will not be redeemed for free donuts.
> (E) Donut Chain's stores are generally very profitable.

5

Step 1: Identify the question.

Which of the following, if true, most strengthens the prediction that Donut Chain's promotion will increase the new store's profitability?	*The language "if true" and "most strengthens the prediction that …" indicates that this is a Strengthen the Argument question. Also, the question stem tells me the conclusion I need to address: the plan will lead to better profitability.*	S A B C D E Ⓒ promo → ↑ prof

Step 2: Deconstruct the argument.

Donut Chain, wishing to increase the profitability of its new store, will place a coupon in the local newspaper offering a free donut with a cup of coffee at its grand opening.	*Donut Chain thinks that giving away a free donut will lead to increased profitability.*	promo = free coupon
Donut Chain calculates that the cost of the advertisement and the free donuts will be more than recouped by the new business generated through the promotion.	*It costs $ to place the ad and give away free donuts, but Donut Chain thinks it'll get enough new business to offset those costs. Still, does that lead to better profitability?*	$ spent < $ new biz
(brainstorm assumptions)	*The argument isn't 100% clear that the profitability part is the conclusion, but the question stem also said so. The author is assuming that giving away a free donut once will lead to increased revenues over time (what if they never come back?), and that will then lead to increased profits (more revenues don't necessarily equal more profits).*	

Step 3: State the goal.

I need to strengthen the claim that a particular plan is going to lead to increased profitability. The plan is to distribute coupons to give away free donuts.

I need to find an answer that makes it a little more likely that this plan will lead to more profits.

Step 4: Work from wrong to right.

(A) Donut Chain has a loyal following in much of the country.	*This is good for Donut Chain. Does that mean it will __increase__ profitability though? No. It's already an established fact. Plus, it only says that Donut Chain enjoys a loyal following in "much" of the country, not necessarily where the new store is located.*	~~A~~
(B) Donut Chain has found that the vast majority of new visitors to its stores become regular customers.	*So if Donut Chain can get people to visit once, they'll usually keep coming back. That sounds pretty good for Donut Chain's plan, which is all about getting people to visit the first time for that free donut.*	<u>B</u>
(C) One donut at Donut Chain costs less than a cup of coffee.	*This tells me nothing about profits or revenues or how much they could sell or anything, really. This doesn't address the argument.*	~~C~~
(D) Most of the copies of the coupon in the local newspaper will not be redeemed for free donuts.	*If this happens, then Donut Chain's plan is really unlikely to work—it spends money on the ads, but never gets the new customers to come in. That __weakens__ the conclusion.*	~~D~~
(E) Donut Chain's stores are generally very profitable.	*It's good that Donut Chain stores are usually profitable; that means this new one is likely to be profitable, too. The conclusion, though, specifically talks about __increasing__ the store's profitability—and the question specifically asks whether __this plan__ will accomplish that goal. This choice looks tempting at first, but it doesn't address whether this plan will increase profitability.*	~~E~~

~~A~~   Ⓑ   ~~C~~   ~~D~~   ~~E~~

Common Trap Answers

One of the most common traps is the **Reverse Logic** answer: the question asks you to strengthen, but a trap answer choice weakens the conclusion instead. You saw an example of this with answer choice (D) in the last problem. These can be especially tricky if you misread the conclusion or otherwise get turned around while evaluating the argument.

Most of the wrong answers will have **No Tie to the Argument**—they will neither strengthen nor weaken the argument. Some of these will be more obviously wrong, but these answers can also be quite tricky. A No Tie trap might address something in a premise without actually affecting the conclusion; answer choice (E) in the last problem is a good example. Notice that it says something positive about Donut Chain, but not anything that addresses the specific chain of logic in the argument.

Strengthen Variant: Fill in the Blank

Contrary to popular belief, Fill in the Blank (FitB) questions are not actually a separate question type; rather, any of the existing question types can be presented in FitB format. In practice, most FitB questions are Strengthen questions; occasionally, these are Inference or Find the Assumption questions. (Out of 16 FitB questions in *The Official Guide for GMAT Review* and *The Official Guide for GMAT Verbal Review*, 14 are Strengthen, 1 is Find the Assumption, and 1 is Inference.)

Look at an example:

> Which of the following most logically completes the argument below?
>
> XYZ Industries sells both a premium line of televisions and a basic line. The higher-end line sells at a 20% premium over the basic line and accounts for about half of the company's revenues. The company has announced that it will stop producing premium televisions and sell only the basic line in the future. This plan will help to improve profitability, since _____.

Right away, you'll notice that there is no question stem after the argument—but there is a question above. The location of the question stem (and the blank at the end of the argument) indicates that you have the FitB structure. But which type of question is it?

The clue to help you identify the question will be just before the blank. In the vast majority of these problems, the word "since" or "because" will be just before the blank, in which case you have a Strengthen question.

The author claims that "this plan will help to improve profitability." As with any Strengthen question, your task is to find an answer that will make this claim more likely to be true.

For the above example, for instance, a correct answer might read:

> premium televisions costs 40% more to produce and market than do basic televisions

If the company charges 20% more for a premium television, but has to pay 40% more to produce and market it, then it's more likely that the company makes less money on premium televisions than it does on basic ones. (This is not an absolute slam dunk, but that's okay. You just have to make the argument more likely to be valid.) Given this, the plan to drop the premium televisions and sell only the basic ones is more likely to improve profitability, strengthening the author's case.

On some FitB questions, the correct answer reinforces or even restates a premise already given in the argument. Most of the time, though, the correct answer will introduce a new premise, as with regular Strengthen questions. Either way, the result will be the same: the answer will make the author's argument at least a little more likely to be true.

Negatively Worded Claims

Many FitB questions introduce a negatively worded twist. Take a look at this variation on the original argument:

> Which of the following most logically completes the argument below?
>
> XYZ Industries sells both a premium line of televisions and a basic line. The higher-end line sells at a 20% premium but also costs 40% more to produce and market. Producing more televisions from the basic line, however, will not necessarily help to improve profitability, since _____.

This is still a Strengthen question because the word "since" is just before the underline. The conclusion is that last sentence: a particular plan will *not* necessarily help to improve profitability. Why? Consider this possible correct answer:

> the market for basic televisions is shrinking

In other words, producing more TVs doesn't necessarily mean the company can *sell* more TVs, and it would have to sell them in order to make money. If the market for basic TVs is shrinking, then producing more of those TVs won't necessarily be beneficial for the company's profitability.

If you see "since _____" in a FitB question, your goal is to strengthen the conclusion that comes before, even if that conclusion contains a "not" or is otherwise worded negatively.

Alternative Wording

The "since _____" or "because _____" variations are the two most common ways in which Complete the Argument questions can be presented. There are a few alternative examples, however, that might pop up. Students aiming for 90th percentile or higher on the Verbal section may want to be prepared for these rare variations; otherwise, it's fine to skip this section.

The rare variants will still typically include the conclusion or claim in the final sentence with the blank, but the "lead-in" wording to the blank will be different, signaling a different question type.

"Lead-in" Wording	Answer Choice Should	Question Type
if (some claim is true), "it should be expected that" _____	represent something that must be true given the information in the argument	Inference
(in order for some claim to be true) "it must be shown that" _____	represent something that must be true given the information in the argument	Inference
(something is true) "assuming that" _____	articulate an assumption used to draw the conclusion	Find the Assumption

Common Trap Answers

The common trap answers will mirror the trap answers given on the regular question type. For example, if the question is a Strengthen, then you should expect to see the same trap answers that you see on regular Strengthen questions: **Reverse Logic** (weakens rather than strengthens) and **No Tie to the Argument**.

Weaken the Argument Questions

Weaken the Argument questions ask you to find a *new* piece of information that, if added to the existing argument, will make the argument less likely to be valid. Your goal, then, is to *attack* the argument. The correct answer will generally attack some assumption made by the author.

Most Weaken question stems contain either the word "weaken" or a synonym of it. You will also typically see the phrase "if true" and question stems similar to these examples:

- Which of the following, if true, most seriously weakens the conclusion? (variant: which is a weakness?)
- Which of the following, if true, would cast the most serious doubt on the validity of the argument? (variant: raise the most serious doubt regarding)
- Which of the following, if true, most strongly calls into question the author's conclusion?
- Which of the following, if true, most seriously undermines the mayor's claim?

Sometimes, the question stem will contain more unusual language, such as the words in quotes below:

- find a "disadvantage" or what is "damaging" to the argument
- a plan is "ill-suited" or otherwise unlikely to succeed
- find a "criticism" of the argument

Now try the same short argument about QuestCorp from earlier in the chapter, but with a different question stem and answers:

> At QuestCorp, many employees have quit recently and taken jobs with a competitor. Shortly before the employees quit, QuestCorp lost its largest client. Clearly, the employees were no longer confident in QuestCorp's long-term viability.
>
> Which of the following, if true, most seriously undermines the claim that concerns about QuestCorp's viability caused the employees to quit?
>
> (A) A new competitor in the same town provides health insurance for its employees, a benefit that QuestCorp lacks.
> (B) QuestCorp is unlikely to be able to replace the lost revenue via either an increase in existing client sales or the attraction of new clients.
> (C) Many prospective hires who have interviewed with QuestCorp ultimately accepted jobs with other companies.

The question stem indicates that this is a Weaken question. In your mind or on your paper, the argument core might look like this:

therefore

lost client,   ⇒   quit b/c concerns about:
ppl quit   success

(premise)   (conclusion)

As always, make sure that you understand what the argument is trying to say. The author claims that losing this client caused employees to lose confidence in QuestCorp, leading them to quit. The author is assuming that losing this one client was serious enough to result in a major problem for the company. Is that necessarily the case?

Remind yourself of your goal:

> *This is a Weaken question, so I have to find some evidence that makes it <u>less</u> likely that people quit for that reason. That could be because it wasn't really a big problem, or it could be that there was some other reason that people quit.*

(A) A new competitor in the same town provides health insurance for its employees, a benefit that QuestCorp lacks.	*The argument claims that people left for one reason, but this answer actually provides an alternative. Maybe people quit because they could get better benefits at the other company. This would weaken the claim that people quit specifically because of concerns over QuestCorp's viability as a company.*	A̰
(B) QuestCorp is unlikely to be able to replace the lost revenue via either an increase in existing client sales or the attraction of new clients.	*So QuestCorp lost its largest client, which means a loss of revenue, and the company probably can't find a way to make up that revenue through other sales. That definitely reinforces the problem described in the argument. This actually strengthens the argument; that's the opposite of what I want.*	B̶
(C) Many prospective hires who have interviewed with QuestCorp ultimately accepted jobs with other companies.	*Hmm. "Prospective hires" are not <u>employees</u>. I was asked to weaken the part about employees losing confidence in QuestCorp. I could speculate that maybe something is wrong with the company if people take other jobs...but the answer doesn't even tell me <u>why</u> these people took other jobs. Maybe QuestCorp rejected them!*	C̶

Ⓐ   B̶   C̶

The correct answer is (**A**).

Answer (B) repeats the common Reverse Logic trap discussed earlier: it strengthens the argument. Answer (C) attempts to distract you by talking about a different part of the argument—perhaps you'll reason that, if interviewees took different jobs, then they didn't believe QuestCorp was a good company. You have no idea why these prospective hires ended up working for another company, though—it's entirely possible that QuestCorp didn't extend a job offer to these people.

Note that the problem used the exact same answer choice (C) for both the Strengthen and Weaken versions of this QuestCorp problem. If a choice is irrelevant to the argument, as choice (C) was, then it doesn't matter whether you're asked to strengthen or weaken the argument. An irrelevant choice doesn't affect the argument at all.

Try this full example:

> The national infrastructure for airport runways and air traffic control requires immediate expansion to accommodate the increase in smaller private planes. To help fund this expansion, the Federal Aviation Authority has proposed a fee for all air travelers. However, this fee would be unfair, as it would impose costs on all travelers to benefit only the few who utilize the new private planes.
>
> Which of the following, if true, would cast the most doubt on the claim that the proposed fee would be unfair?
>
> (A) The existing national airport infrastructure benefits all air travelers.
> (B) The fee, if imposed, will have a negligible impact on the overall volume of air travel.
> (C) The expansion would reduce the number of delayed flights resulting from small private planes congesting runways.
> (D) Travelers who use small private planes are almost uniformly wealthy or traveling on business.
> (E) A substantial fee would need to be imposed in order to pay for the expansion costs.

Step 1: Identify the question

Which of the following, if true, would cast the most doubt on the claim that the proposed fee would be unfair?	*The language "cast the most doubt on the claim" indicates that this is a Weaken question. Attack: the proposed fee would be unfair.*	W A B C D E Ⓒ fee = unfair

Step 2: Deconstruct the argument

The national infrastructure for airport runways and air traffic control requires immediate expansion to accommodate the increase in smaller, private planes.	*This is written as a fact and appears to be stating something that has already been established; I'm guessing it's background info, not the conclusion, but I'm not 100% sure.*	To handle more small priv planes → must expand infra
To help fund this expansion, the Federal Aviation Authority has proposed a fee for all air travelers.	*Okay, here's a plan. It could be the conclusion. The FAA wants to charge a fee to pay for the expansion.*	FAA: fee → fund exp
However, this fee would be unfair, as it would impose costs on all travelers to benefit only the few who utilize the new private planes.	*Change of direction! The author disagrees with the plan, claiming it's unfair. The author's reasoning: everyone would have to pay the fee, but only a few people would benefit.* *Why wouldn't everyone benefit? If there's more space, then all the planes will be able to take off more quickly. The author is assuming the benefit is only for the people flying in small planes.*	BUT fee = unfair b/c all pay to benef few

Step 3: State the goal.

The airports are congested because there are so many small planes, and the FAA wants to charge a fee to expand the airports. The author claims that this is unfair because the fee would be paid by all but the expansion would only benefit a few.

I want to weaken the author's conclusion, so I need to find some reason why it really isn't unfair. One possibility: maybe more people will benefit than just the "small plane" people.

Step 4: Work from wrong to right.

(A) The existing national airport infrastructure benefits all air travelers.	*This sounds like what I was thinking before—everyone benefits, so why is it unfair for everyone to pay? Great; I'll leave it in.*	A̲
(B) The fee, if imposed, will have a negligible impact on the overall volume of air travel.	*A "negligible impact" means it won't really change anything. The fee won't change the volume of planes trying to fly…but that was never the plan. The plan was to raise money to expand the infrastructure—then they'll be able to handle more volume. This answer doesn't address the right thing.*	B

(C) The expansion would reduce the number of delayed flights resulting from small private planes congesting runways.	*Hmm. This is another potential benefit for everyone—a reduction in the number of flight delays. I'll leave this one in, too.*	C̲
(D) Travelers who use small private planes are almost uniformly wealthy or traveling on business.	*That's nice for them, but what does it have to do with this argument? Maybe you could say "so they can afford to pay more," but that isn't the point of the argument. The point of the argument is that it's unfair to make the regular travelers pay for something that doesn't benefit them (according to the author).*	D̶
(E) A substantial fee would need to be imposed in order to pay for the expansion costs.	*So the fee would have to be pretty large. If anything, doesn't that make it even more unfair? Though, actually, I don't think it really addresses the fairness at all. Either it is fair, in which case the size of the fee doesn't matter, or it isn't fair…in which case the size of the fee still doesn't matter.*	E̶
Examine (A) and (C) again.	*Compare choices (A) and (C). Both say that this expansion would benefit everyone…wait a second. Choice (C) does explicitly mention the expansion, but (A) says "the existing…infrastructure." Existing? Of course, the existing structure benefits everyone who uses it—the argument isn't about that. It's about whether the <u>expansion</u> would benefit everyone. Only choice (C) actually says that; I missed that the first time around.*	A̶ Ⓒ

A̲   B̶   Ⓒ   D̶   E̶

Common Trap Answers

Weaken questions contain the same kind of common trap answers that show up on Strengthen questions.

One of the trickiest types is the **Reverse Logic** trap: the question asks you to weaken, but a trap answer choice strengthens the argument instead. You will also again see the **No Tie to the Argument** traps—choices that might discuss something in a premise but don't affect the argument.

The most tempting wrong answer in the last problem, answer choice (A), is actually a No Tie trap. Almost everything in the choice was addressing the right thing but one word made it wrong: "existing." The conclusion was about the future infrastructure, after an expansion, so limiting the answer to the existing infrastructure meant that the information didn't affect the conclusion after all.

MANHATTAN
PREP

EXCEPT Questions

Assumption Family questions may also be presented in a "negative" form that is commonly referred to as EXCEPT questions.

A regular Weaken question might read:

> Which of the following, if true, most seriously weakens the conclusion?

An EXCEPT Weaken question might read:

> Each of the following, if true, weakens the conclusion EXCEPT:

What is the difference in wording between those two questions?

The first one indicates that one answer choice, and only one, weakens the argument. You want to pick that choice.

The second one indicates that four answer choices weaken the argument. These four are all wrong answers. What about the fifth answer—what does that one do?

Many people assume that the fifth one must do the opposite: strengthen the argument. *This is not necessarily true.* The fifth one certainly does not weaken the argument, but it may not strengthen the argument either. It might have no impact whatsoever on the argument.

For these negatively worded questions, use the "odd one out" strategy. Four of the answer choices will do the same thing; in the case of the above example, four answers will weaken the argument. The fifth choice, the correct one, will do something else. It doesn't matter whether the fifth one strengthens the argument or does nothing—all that matters is that it is the "odd one out," the one that does *not* weaken. In order to keep track of the four similar answers versus the "odd one out," label the choices as you assess them with an S for Strengthen, a W for Weaken, and an N for Neutral or "does Nothing."

Try this example:

> Supporters of a costly new Defense Advanced Research Projects Agency (DARPA) initiative assert that the project will benefit industrial companies as well as the military itself. In many instances, military research has resulted in technologies that have fueled corporate development and growth, and this pattern can be expected to continue.
>
> Each of the following, if true, serves to weaken the argument above EXCEPT:
>
> (A) The research initiative will occupy many talented scientists, many of whom would otherwise have worked for private corporations.
> (B) In the past decade, DARPA has adopted an increasingly restrictive stance regarding the use of intellectual property resulting from its research.
> (C) If the DARPA initiative hadn't been approved, much of the funding would instead have been directed toward tax breaks for various businesses.
> (D) At any given time, DARPA is conducting a wide variety of costly research projects.
> (E) The research initiative is focused on specific defense mechanisms that would be ineffective for private corporations.

5

Step 1: Identify the question.

Each of the following, if true, serves to weaken the argument above EXCEPT:	*The language "serves to weaken" indicates that this is a weaken question. The word EXCEPT indicates that the four wrong answers will weaken, and I want to pick the "odd one out" answer.*	WEx A B C D E

Step 2: Deconstruct the argument.

Supporters of a costly new Defense Advanced Research Projects Agency (DARPA) initiative assert that the project will benefit industrial companies as well as the military itself.	*The supporters of DARPA think that this costly project will be good for companies and for the military.*	ⓒ Supporters: Costly proj will benef co's & mil

MANHATTAN
PREP

In many instances, military research has resulted in technologies that have fueled corporate development and growth, and this pattern can be expected to continue.	*Research has helped companies in the past, and the author claims this will keep happening in the future. That all supports the claim of the supporterss: that the specific DARPA project will be beneficial for companies.*	past: mil research → techs help co's, will cont

Step 3: State the goal.

In the past, military research has helped companies, and the claim is that this DARPA project will also help companies.

I want to find four answers that weaken the argument. The answer that doesn't weaken—the odd one out—is the correct answer.

Step 4: Work from wrong to right.

(A) The research initiative will occupy many talented scientists, many of whom would otherwise have worked for private corporations.	*This benefits the military and specifically does not benefit the companies. That does weaken the idea that companies will benefit.*	A̶ W
(B) In the past decade, DARPA has adopted an increasingly restrictive stance regarding the use of intellectual property resulting from its research.	*Hmm. "Restrictive" makes it sound like DARPA doesn't let others use its research as much. If that's the case, then that would weaken the idea that companies will benefit. I'm not totally sure that's what this means though—the wording is tricky—so I'm going to give this a question mark come back to it later.*	B W?
(C) If the DARPA initiative hadn't been approved, much of the funding would instead have been directed toward tax breaks for various businesses.	*A tax break is a good thing, This choice is saying that the funding for the DARPA project would instead have been spent on tax breaks, which is a definite benefit. So not giving those tax breaks is a bad thing for the companies; this does weaken the argument.*	C̶ W
(D) At any given time, DARPA is conducting a wide variety of costly research projects.	*This choice talks about all research projects DARPA is conducting. Hmm. The argument makes a claim only about one specific project. Does this information make that claim more or less likely to be valid? I can't really see how it affects the argument's conclusion at all.*	D N

5

(E) The research initiative is focused on specific defense mechanisms that would be ineffective for private corporations.	*The key here is the language "ineffective for private corporations." If the private companies can't make effective use of the results of this particular research, then that weakens the claim that the DARPA research will benefit companies.*	E̶ W
Examine (B) and (D) again.	*I need to compare answers (B) and (D). I thought (B) might weaken a little bit, and I thought (D) didn't do anything to the argument. Between those two, I should choose the one that doesn't weaken at all, so I'm going to choose choice (D).*	B̶ Ⓓ W N

The correct answer is choice (**D**).

The biggest "trap answer" on an EXCEPT question is simply to forget halfway through that you're working on an EXCEPT question. If this happens, you might accidentally pick a Weaken answer, or pick the answer that you think *most* weakens the argument. The "W" labels under your weaken answers will help to remind you that multiple answers weaken, so that is not what you want to pick.

Cheat Sheets

Strengthen the Argument Cheat Sheet

Identify
the Question

Common:	*strengthen*
	support
	if true
For Fill in the Blank, *because* or *since* before the blank	
Less common:	*if feasible*
	best basis or *best reason*

Deconstruct
the Argument

Find:	Conclusion, premises
Brainstorm:	Assumptions, gaps in argument

State the **Goal**

A new piece of information that makes the argument more likely to be valid

Work from
Wrong to **Right**

Right:	Makes the argument stronger
Wrong:	Reverse Logic (makes conclusion weaker)
	No Tie to Argument

Photocopy this page and keep it with the review sheets you're creating as you study. Better yet, use this page as a guide to create your own review sheet—you'll remember the material better if you write it down yourself.

Note: Fill in the Blank is almost always Strengthen, because the blank is usually preceded by *since* or *because*. When in doubt, assume that the question type is Strengthen.

Weaken the Argument Cheat Sheet

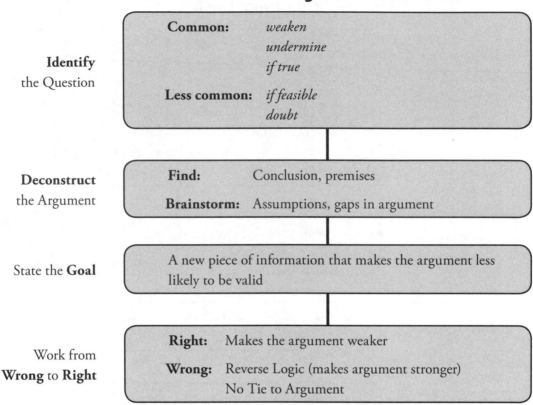

Identify
the Question

Common:	*weaken*
	undermine
	if true
Less common:	*if feasible*
	doubt

Deconstruct
the Argument

Find: Conclusion, premises

Brainstorm: Assumptions, gaps in argument

State the **Goal**

A new piece of information that makes the argument less likely to be valid

Work from
Wrong to **Right**

Right: Makes the argument weaker

Wrong: Reverse Logic (makes argument stronger)
          No Tie to Argument

Photocopy this page and keep it with the review sheets you're creating as you study. Better yet, use this page as a guide to create your own review sheet—you'll remember the material better if you write it down yourself.

Problem Set

1. *Motor City*

    Which of the following best completes the passage below?

    A nonprofit organization in Motor City has proposed that local college students be given the option to buy half-price monthly passes for the city's public transportation system. The nonprofit claims that this plan will reduce air pollution in Motor City while increasing profits for the city's public transportation system. However, this plan is unlikely to meet its goals, since _____.

    (A) most college students in Motor City view public transportation as unsafe

    (B) most college students in Motor City view public transportation as prohibitively expensive

    (C) college students typically do not have the 9-to-5 schedules of most workers, and can thus be expected to ride public transportation at times when there are plenty of empty seats

    (D) a bus produces more air pollution per mile than does a car

    (E) a large proportion of the college students in Motor City live off campus

2. *Smithtown Theatre*

    The Smithtown Theatre, which stages old plays, has announced an expansion that will double its capacity along with its operating costs. The theatre is only slightly profitable at present. In addition, all of the current customers live in Smithtown, and the population of the town is not expected to increase in the next several years. Thus, the expansion of the Smithtown Theatre will prove unprofitable.

    Which of the following, if true, would most seriously weaken the argument?

    (A) A large movie chain plans to open a new multiplex location in Smithtown later this year.

    (B) Concession sales in the Smithtown Theatre comprise a substantial proportion of the theatre's revenues.

    (C) Many recent arrivals to Smithtown are students who are less likely to attend the Smithtown Theatre than are older residents.

    (D) The expansion would allow the Smithtown Theatre to stage larger, more popular shows that will attract customers from neighboring towns.

    (E) The Board of the Smithtown Theatre often solicits input from residents of the town when choosing which shows to stage.

3. *Books and Coffee*

The owners of a book store and a nearby coffee shop have decided to combine their businesses. Both owners believe that this merger will increase the number of customers and therefore the gross revenue, because customers who come for one reason may also decide to purchase something else.

Which of the following, if true, most weakens the owners' conclusion that a merger will increase revenue?

(A) Books and drinks can both be considered impulse purchases; often, they are purchased by customers without forethought.

(B) Profit margins at a coffee shop are generally significantly higher than profit margins at a book store.

(C) People who are able to read the first chapter of a book before buying are more likely to decide to buy the book.

(D) A large majority of the book store's current customer base already frequents the coffee shop.

(E) A combination book store and coffee shop that opened in a neighboring city last year has already earned higher than expected profits.

4. *Digital Coupons*

The redemption rate for e-mailed coupons is far lower than that for traditionally distributed paper coupons. One factor is the "digital divide"—those who might benefit the most from using coupons, such as homemakers, the elderly, and those in low-income households, are less likely to have the knowledge or equipment necessary to go online and receive coupons.

Which of the following, if true, does the most to support the claim that the digital divide is responsible for lower electronic coupon redemption rates?

(A) Computers are available for free in libraries, schools, and community centers.

(B) The redemption rate of ordinary coupons is particularly high among elderly and low-income people who do not know how to use computers.

(C) Many homes, including those of elderly and low-income people, do not have high-speed internet connections.

(D) More homemakers than elderly people would use computers if they had access to them.

(E) The redemption rate for coupons found on the internet has risen in the last five years.

5. *Teacher Compensation*

Traditionally, public school instructors have been compensated according to seniority. Recently, educational experts have criticized the system as one that rewards lackadaisical teaching and reduces motivation to excel. Instead, these experts argue that, to retain exceptional teachers and maintain quality instruction, teachers should receive salaries or bonuses based on performance rather than seniority.

Which of the following, if true, most weakens the argument of the educational experts?

(A) Some teachers express that financial compensation is not the only factor contributing to job satisfaction and teaching performance.

(B) School districts will develop their own unique compensation structures that may differ greatly from those of other school districts.

(C) Upon leaving the teaching profession, many young, effective teachers cite a lack of opportunity for more rapid financial advancement as a primary factor in the decision to change careers.

(D) In school districts that have implemented pay for performance compensation structures, standardized test scores have dramatically increased.

(E) A merit-based system that bases compensation on teacher performance reduces collaboration, which is an integral component of quality instruction.

6. *Farmsley Center*

The Farmsley Film and Performing Arts Center was built three years ago in downtown Metropolis. A recent study shows that, on average, a person who attends a show at the Farmsley Center spends $96 at other downtown businesses on the day of the show.

Each of the following, if true, would cast serious doubt on the claim that the Farmsley Center is a significant driver of the economic success of downtown Metropolis EXCEPT:

(A) People who do not attend a Farmsley Center show spend $103 on average when shopping in the downtown area.

(B) Restaurants near the Farmsley Center tend to be more expensive than restaurants in other areas of the downtown.

(C) Most of the people who attend films or performances at the Farmsley Center do so because they are already in the area to shop.

(D) Tax revenues from all products and services sold in the downtown area have changed little in five years.

(E) Another downtown theatre is the only one large enough to show popular, newly released Hollywood films.

5

7. *Machu Picchu*

In 2001 the Peruvian government began requiring tourists to buy permits to hike the Inca Trail to the ancient city of Machu Picchu. Only 500 people per day are now allowed to hike the Inca Trail, whereas before 2001 daily visitors numbered in the thousands. The Peruvian government claims that this permit program has successfully prevented deterioration of archaeological treasures along the Inca Trail.

Which of the following, if true, most strengthens the argument above?

(A) Since 2001, Incan ruins similar to Machu Picchu but without a visitor limit have disintegrated at a significantly greater rate than those on the Inca Trail.

(B) Villages near Machu Picchu have experienced declines in income, as fewer tourists buy fewer craft goods and refreshments.

(C) Many of the funds from the sale of Inca Trail permits are used to hire guards for archaeological sites without permit programs.

(D) Since 2001, tourist guides along the Inca Trail have received 50% to 100% increases in take-home pay.

(E) The total number of tourists in Peru has risen substantially since 2001, even as the number of tourists hiking the Inca Trail has remained constant.

8. *Digital Video Recorders*

Advertising Executive: More than 10 million households now own digital video recorders that can fast-forward over television commercials; approximately 75% of these households fast-forward over at least one commercial per 30-minute program. Because television commercials are not as widely watched as they used to be, they are much less cost-effective today.

Which of the following is required in order for the advertising executive to claim that television commercials are less cost-effective today?

(A) Product placement within television programs is a viable alternative to traditional television commercials.

(B) The television programs preferred by consumers without digital video recorders are similar to those preferred by consumers with the devices.

(C) Prior to the advent of digital video recorders, very few television viewers switched channels or left the room when commercials began.

(D) The cost-effectiveness of television advertising is based less upon how many people watch a particular commercial and more upon the appropriateness of the demographic.

(E) Many companies find it difficult to determine the exact return on investment for television commercials.

9. *APR*

CEO: Over the past several years, we have more than doubled our revenues but profits have steadily declined because an increasing number of customers have failed to pay their balances. In order to compensate for these higher default rates, we will increase the interest charged on outstanding balances from an annual percentage rate (APR) of 9.5% to an APR of 12%. This increase will be sufficient to compensate for the current rate of defaults and allow us to increase our profits.

Which of the following statements, if true, would most seriously undermine a plan to increase interest rates in order to spur profitable growth?

(A) Many other companies have experienced a similar trend in their default rates.

(B) The company's operating expenses are above the industry average and can be substantially reduced, thus increasing margins.

(C) The increase in default rates was due to a rise in unemployment, but unemployment rates are expected to drop in the coming months.

(D) The proposed increase in the APR will, alone, more than double the company's profit margins.

(E) An increase in the APR charged on credit card balances often results in higher rates of default.

10. *Jupiter vs. Mars*

Scientists suspect that Europa, a moon orbiting Jupiter, may contain living organisms. However, the government recently scrapped an unmanned science mission to Europa and replaced it with a project aimed at landing an astronaut on Mars. Polls show that the public is far more fascinated by space travel than by discovering life elsewhere in the universe. Critics argue that the government's decision-making process places a greater emphasis on popularity than it does on the importance of scientific research.

Which of the following, if true, would most strengthen a contention by the government that the new project is a better use of its funds?

(A) In the first year of the project, the government will spend 30% of its total budget on developing a space shuttle that can travel to Mars; that figure is expected to drop to 0% after five years.

(B) The government cannot be absolutely certain of the chances for success of either project.

(C) Some scientists are convinced that a mission to Europa would add immeasurably to our understanding of the universe.

(D) A new telescope that has just become available to scientists promises to yield more information than the planned mission to Europa was designed to provide.

(E) Most people feel that a shuttle to Mars is the next logical step in the development of a system that will allow humans to travel even further in the solar system.

5

11. *Deep-brain Stimulation*

Which of the following most logically completes the argument given below?

Deep-brain stimulation is a new technique for combating severe depression. In a recent experiment, electrodes were implanted into the brains of six patients who had not responded to any currently approved treatment for depression. When an electrical current to the electrodes was switched on, four of the patients reported feeling a dramatic reduction in depressive symptoms. The long-term prospects of the new treatment are not promising, however, because _____.

(A) other treatments for depression may also be effective

(B) the other two patients reported only a slight reduction of depressive symptoms during the treatment

(C) deep-brain stimulation relies on the expertise of highly skilled physicians

(D) when the electrical current is interrupted, the effects of the treatment are reversed

(E) in a subsequent experiment, a one-hour treatment with the electrodes resulted in a sustained remission from depression in the four patients for six months

Solutions

1. Motor City: The correct answer is **(A)**.

Step 1: Identify the question.

Which of the following best completes the passage below ?	*The question appears before the argument, and the argument contains a blank at the end. Both of these things indicate that this is a Complete the Argument question.*	CA A B C D E

Step 2: Deconstruct the argument.

A nonprofit organization in Motor City has proposed that local college students be given the option to buy half-price monthly passes for the city's public transportation system.	*This is a fact—the organization has proposed this plan.*	Nonprof: give coll stud 1/2 off pub trans
The nonprofit claims that this plan will reduce air pollution in Motor City while increasing profits for the city's public transportation system.	*Okay, the nonprofit claims something, but I'm not labeling this the conclusion, because the conclusion is supposed to be in the final sentence of CA questions.*	→ ↓ air poll, ↑ prof
However, this plan is unlikely to meet its goals, since _____.	*This is the conclusion. The author thinks the plan won't work. Why?*	Ⓒ BUT unlikely to work

Step 3: State the goal.

The author believes that the nonprofit's plan is not going to work, and I need to find a reason why. The plan is to let college students buy public transportation passes for half price in order to reduce air pollution and increase profits.

Step 4: Work from wrong to right.

(A) most college students in Motor City view public transportation as unsafe	*If this is the case, then the students wouldn't want to use public transport at all, even if they were given a discount. That would make the plan unlikely to succeed. This might be it!*	A̰
(B) most college students in Motor City view public transportation as prohibitively expensive	*If they don't use public transport specifically because it's too expensive, then giving the students a discount is likely to make them use public transport more. This makes the plan more likely to succeed, not less likely.*	B̶
(C) college students typically do not have the 9-to-5 schedules of most workers, and can thus be expected to ride public transportation at times when there are plenty of empty seats	*If this were true, it'd be good news for the public transport's profits—the students would be filling what are currently empty seats.*	C̶
(D) a bus produces more air pollution per mile than does a car	*At first, this sounds good—if a bus produces more air pollution than a car, then using more buses would create more air pollution, which would hurt the plan. But the plan isn't to use more buses; it's to put more people on the already-running buses. Plus, a car typically holds only 1 or 2 people. If 10 people stop using cars and take 1 bus instead, air pollution may indeed be decreased.*	D̶
(E) a large proportion of the college students in Motor City live off campus	*This makes it likely that the students need some method of transportation to get to school—if they're using cars now and switch to buses, then the plan just might work.*	E̶

Ⓐ   B̶   C̶   D̶   E̶

2. Smithtown Theatre: The correct answer is **(D)**.

Step 1: Identify the question.

Which of the following, if true, would most seriously weaken the argument?	*The words "if true" and "weaken" tell me that this is a Weaken question.*	W A B C D E

MANHATTAN
PREP

Step 2: Deconstruct the argument.

The Smithtown Theatre, which stages old plays, has announced an expansion that will double its capacity along with its operating costs.	*They have a plan. It's future, so it could be the conclusion, but I'm guessing there'll be more of a claim like "The theatre will (or will not) be successful with its plan" or something like that.*	Theatre: expand to ↑↑ cap & cost
The theatre is only slightly profitable at present.	*This is a fact. I wonder: if the theatre expands, will it get enough new business to continue covering costs?*	Now: barely prof
In addition, all of the current customers live in Smithtown, and the population of the town is not expected to increase in the next several years.	*The first half is a fact; the second half is a future predication. So far, the case for the theatre's new plan doesn't sound very good.*	Cust live in S, prob won't be more from S
Thus, the expansion of the Smithtown Theatre will prove unprofitable.	*Okay, here's the conclusion. The author thinks the plan will fail and provides some pieces of evidence to support that claim.*	Ⓒ theatre expansion unprof

Step 3: State the goal.

The theatre has a plan to expand but the author claims that the plan will fail because the theatre is only barely profitable right now and it doesn't seem like there are a lot more opportunities to get new customers.

I want something that will weaken the author's claim. I have to be careful here: weaken the idea that the plan will fail. I'm not weakening the plan itself—in fact, weakening the author's claim could well mean strengthening the idea that the plan will work!

Step 4: Work from wrong to right.

(A) A large movie chain plans to open a new multiplex location in Smithtown later this year.	*I don't think what another business does will matter. If anything, you'd have to say that the new movie theatre would take business from the theatre, which would strengthen the author's claim that the theatre will fail.*	A̶
(B) Concession sales in the Smithtown Theatre comprise a substantial proportion of the theatre's revenues.	*How would this change if the theatre expanded? That still depends upon whether they can get more people to come to the theatre, so this doesn't really tell me anything new.*	B̶
(C) Many recent arrivals to Smithtown are students who are less likely to attend the Smithtown Theatre than are older residents.	*So the new people moving to town are people who aren't likely to start going to the theatre. That strengthens the author's claim that ST's expansion is going to fail. Reverse Logic trap!*	C̶
(D) The expansion would allow the Smithtown Theatre to stage larger, more popular shows that will attract patrons from neighboring towns.	*Hmm. This basically means that the expansion would attract a greater audience—that helps! If they have more people, they can fill the larger theatre and make more money. This one is looking good as a weakener for the claim that the expansion will fail.*	D
(E) The Board of the Smithtown Theatre often solicits input from residents of the town when choosing which shows to stage.	*This is how they do things now. Would it stay the same, or change when they expand? I have no idea. This doesn't tell me that some new thing will happen that might make it more likely for the plan to succeed; it just talks about how things are already done.*	E̶

A̶   B̶   C̶   E̶

3. Books and Coffee: The correct answer is **(D)**.

Step 1: Identify the question.

Which of the following, if true, most weakens the owners' conclusion that a merger will increase revenue?	*The words "if true" and "weakens" tell me that this is a Weaken question. Further, I now know the conclusion: some merger will result in increased revenue.*	W A B C D E Ⓒ merger → ↑ rev

Step 2: Deconstruct the argument.

The owners of a book store and a nearby coffee shop have decided to combine their businesses.	*This is a fact; they have already made this decision, although it sounds like they haven't actually merged yet.*	Book + coffee combining
Both owners believe that this merger will increase the number of customers and therefore the gross revenue,	*This is the same thing the Q stem said: the merger will increase revenue.*	Will → ↑ cust, rev
because customers who come for one reason may also decide to purchase something else.	*According to the owners, the individual customers of each store will end up buying both books and coffee, so there'll be more customers for both, which means more revenue for both. That's assuming, of course, that these customers weren't already going to both stores to buy stuff.*	b/c cross-sell

Step 3: State the goal.

The owners think that merging will lead to increased revenue because it'll increase the number of customers and the customers will buy more stuff. This assumes that the same customers weren't already going to both stores and buying stuff.

This is a Weaken question, so I need to find something that will make the conclusion less likely to be valid.

Step 4: Work from wrong to right.

(A) Books and drinks can both be considered impulse purchases; often, they are purchased by customers without forethought.	*This could be a reason why people would buy more. If they normally just buy coffee but see a book they like, maybe they'll be more likely to buy. That would strengthen the plan to merge, but I want to weaken the plan. Reverse Logic trap!*	A̶
(B) Profit margins at a coffee shop are generally significantly higher than profit margins at a book store.	*That might make the coffee shop owner not want to merge, but it doesn't address the revenue side of the equation at all—and the conclusion has to do with revenues, not profits.*	B̶
(C) People who are able to read the first chapter of a book before buying are more likely to decide to buy the book.	*This helps the owners' argument again! If I can sit there and read while having my coffee, then I'm more likely to buy the book, which would increase revenues.*	C̶
(D) A large majority of the book store's current customer base already frequents the coffee shop.	*Let's see. Most of the people who shop at the book store also already go to the coffee shop. That's not so good for the owner's plan—it means that they're not going to pick up as many new customers as I might have thought before.*	D̰
(E) A combination book store and coffee shop that opened in a neighboring city last year has already earned higher than expected profits.	*Two problems here. One, the author's not talking about the same book store and coffee shop. Two, this choice talks about profits, not revenues.*	E̶

A̶   B̶   C̶   Ⓓ   E̶

4. Digital Coupons: The correct answer is **(B)**.

Step 1: Identify the question.

Which of the following, if true, does the most to support the claim that the digital divide is responsible for lower electronic coupon redemption rates?	*The language "if true" and "support the claim" tell me that this is a Strengthen question. The question also indicates the conclusion: something called the "digital divide" causes electronic coupons not to be used as much.*	S A B C D E ⓒDig divide → ↓ use e-coup

Step 2: Deconstruct the argument.

The redemption rate for e-mailed coupons is far lower than that for traditionally distributed paper coupons.	*This is a fact. For some reason, e-mailed coupons don't get used as much as paper coupons.*	e-coup redeem less than paper
One factor is the "digital divide"—those who might benefit the most from using coupons, such as homemakers, the elderly, and those in low-income households, are less likely to have the knowledge or equipment necessary to go online and receive coupons.	*Okay, so the people who would typically use coupons are less likely to be able to get them electronically—they have to use the paper coupons instead. This doesn't really articulate the conclusion that well—the question stem did, so I'm going to add something here*	Dig Divide: ppl who use coups can't get them online

Step 3: State the goal.

The author claims that the "digital divide" causes lower use of the e-coupons because people who use coupons aren't as likely to have access to e-coupons.

I need to find something that makes this more likely to be true.

Step 4: Work from wrong to right.

(A) Computers are available for free in libraries, schools, and community centers.	*If this is true, then people who don't have computers can still use them. Maybe they could even take classes to learn how to use them! If anything, this weakens the author's claim.*	~~A~~
(B) The redemption rate of ordinary coupons is particularly high among elderly and low-income people who do not know how to use computers.	*At first glance, I thought, "This is just saying what the argument already said, which is weird because usually they don't do that." Then I realized that there was a gap in the argument! The argument only says that these people without computers are the ones who would "benefit the most" from coupons, but it doesn't say that these people actually do use coupons more. This choice tells me that; this strengthens the conclusion.*	~~B~~
(C) Many homes, including those of elderly and low-income people, do not have high-speed internet connections.	*The argument doesn't say that people have to have high-speed connections in order to get coupons. The issue was whether these groups had internet access at all, not how fast the internet access is.*	~~C~~
(D) More homemakers than elderly people would use computers if they had access to them.	*The argument doesn't make any distinction between homemakers and the elderly; rather, they're both equally part of the group of people without easy access to the internet. This is irrelevant.*	~~D~~
(E) The redemption rate for coupons found on the internet has risen in the last five years.	*This means that more people are using electronic coupons today, but the argument doesn't claim that people aren't. Instead, it talks about the fact that paper coupons are still in wider use because some people find it harder to access the electronic coupons. This answer does nothing to affect the conclusion.*	~~E~~

~~A~~ Ⓑ ~~C~~ ~~D~~ ~~E~~

5. Teacher Compensation: The correct answer is **(E)**.

Step 1: Identify the question.

Which of the following, if true, most weakens the argument of the educational experts?	*The language "if true" and "weakens" tells me this is a Weaken question. In addition, the question tells me that I need to look for a reference to "educational experts" because whatever they claim is the conclusion.*	W A B C D E

Step 2: Deconstruct the argument.

Traditionally, public school instructors have been compensated according to seniority.	*Fact: teachers have been getting paid based upon how long they've worked.*	Trad: Pub school teachers = $ by seniority
Recently, educational experts have criticized the system as one that rewards lackadaisical teaching and reduces motivation to excel.	*I guess the experts are implying that teachers don't have to feel motivated to work hard because they know they'll make more money regardless.*	Experts: ↓ motiv
Instead, these experts argue that, to retain exceptional teachers and maintain quality instruction, teachers should receive salaries or bonuses based on performance rather than seniority.	*So the experts want to base compensation on performance, and they claim this will lead to better teachers and instruction. This is the conclusion of the experts' argument.*	Ⓒ Base comp on perform → keep great teachers

Step 3: State the goal.

Teachers normally get paid based on seniority, but these experts want them to be paid based on performance because (according to these experts) the teachers will then be better.

I need to find something that weakens this plan.

Step 4: Work from wrong to right.

(A) Some teachers express that financial compensation is not the only factor contributing to job satisfaction and teaching performance.	*So maybe we should also consider other ways to reward good teachers too, but as long as financial compensation is a factor, then tying compensation to performance might be a good plan. According to this answer, financial compensation is a factor (though not the only one).*	A̶
(B) School districts will develop their own unique compensation structures that may differ greatly from those of other school districts.	*The argument isn't claiming that every school district has to be identical. It just makes a recommendation that compensation be tied to performance in general.*	B̶
(C) Upon leaving the teaching profession, many young, effective teachers cite a lack of opportunity for more rapid financial advancement as a primary factor in the decision to change careers.	*If anything, I think this would strengthen the experts' claim! It shows that teachers do care about the financial side of things and causes some good teachers to leave the profession at a young age.*	C̶
(D) In school districts that have implemented pay for performance compensation structures, standardized test scores have dramatically increased.	*Again, if anything, this makes the experts' plan sound better. Students in the school districts that have already followed the experts' recommendation are doing better on tests!*	D̶
(E) A merit-based system that bases compensation on teacher performance reduces collaboration, which is an integral component of quality instruction.	*The experts' plan has a drawback: it reduces something that is considered an "integral component" of good teaching. If that's true, it could hurt the idea that basing compensation on performance will result in maintaining good instruction.*	E̲

A̶   B̶   C̶   D̶   Ⓔ

6. Farmsley Center: The correct answer is **(B)**.

Step 1: Identify the question.

Each of the following, if true, would cast serious doubt on the claim that the Farmsley Center is a significant driver of the economic success of downtown Metropolis EXCEPT	*The "if true" and "serious doubt" language indicates that this is a Weaken question, and the EXCEPT language indicates that the four wrong answers will weaken the claim.*	WEx A B C D E F-Center → econ success of Metro

Step 2: Deconstruct the argument.

The Farmsley Film and Performing Arts Center was built three years ago in downtown Metropolis.	*This is just a fact. The center was built 3 years ago.*	Built 3 yrs ago
A recent study shows that, on average, a person who attends a show at the Farmsley Center spends $96 at other downtown businesses on the day of the show.	*Interesting. If people who attend a Farmsley Center show also spend $96 other places, then it sounds like the center might be a driver of economic success.*	Ppl spend $96 other places

Step 3: State the goal.

The claim is this center is a significant driver of downtown Metropolis's economic success. The four wrong answers will all weaken this idea. The "odd one out" might strengthen the argument or might do nothing at all.

Step 4: Work from wrong to right.

(A) People who do not attend a Farmsley Center show spend $103 on average when shopping in the downtown area.	*If people spend more at other establishments when not attending a Farmsley Center show, then it's more difficult to claim that the center drives the economic success of the area. This choice weakens the argument.*	A̶ W
(B) Restaurants near the Farmsley Center tend to be more expensive than restaurants in other areas of the downtown.	*At first, this seems like it could weaken, but I don't know why those restaurants are more expensive. Maybe they were already there when the center opened. This choice actually doesn't tell me anything at all about whether this center drives the success of the area.*	B N

(C) Most of the people who attend films or performances at the Farmsley Center do so because they are already in the area to shop.	*If people go to the area first to shop and then just happen to go to the Farmsley Center to see a show, then it sounds like the shops are the drivers of success, not this center. This choice weakens.*	~~C~~ W
(D) Tax revenues from all products and services sold in the downtown area have changed little in five years.	*Farmsley Center opened three years ago. If it were a driver of economic success in the area, then you'd expect more transactions, likely leading to higher tax revenues. If tax revenues haven't changed much, then the idea that this center is driving business is weakened.*	~~D~~ W
(E) Another downtown theatre is the only one large enough to show popular, newly released Hollywood films.	*Maybe the other theatre is a driver of success! If the Farmsley Center has competition and is not actually large enough to show the popular Hollywood films, then it's less likely that this center is a significant driver of the downtown's success.*	~~E~~ W

 ~~A~~ W   (B) N   ~~C~~ W   ~~D~~ W   ~~E~~ W

7. Machu Picchu: The correct answer is (A).

Step 1: Identify the question.

Which of the following, if true, most strengthens the argument above?	*The words "if true" and "strengthens the argument" indicate that this is a Strengthen question.*	SA A B C D E

Step 2: Deconstruct the argument.

In 2001 the Peruvian government began requiring tourists to buy permits to hike the Inca Trail to the ancient city of Machu Picchu.	*This is a fact. People now have to pay to hike the Inca Trail.*	2001 Peru gov: req permits to hike Inca Trail
Only 500 people per day are now allowed to hike the Inca Trail, whereas before 2001 daily visitors numbered in the thousands.	*More facts. Now, only 500 people a day can go; before, there were thousands a day.*	Now: 500/day (old = 000's)

MANHATTAN
PREP

The Peruvian government claims that this permit program has successfully prevented deterioration of archaeological treasures along the Inca Trail.	*Here's the claim: the PG specifically says that the permit program is responsible for preventing deterioration along the trail.*	Ⓒ Gov: permits → ↓ damage

Step 3: State the goal.

The Peruvian government claims that its permit program has been responsible for preventing deterioration along the Inca Trail. The only thing I know about the permit program is that it has reduced the number of people who can visit the trail. So the government is assuming that reducing the number of visitors was the cause, and that if the permit program hadn't been in place, then there would have been deterioration.

I need to find something that makes this more likely to be valid.

Step 4: Work from wrong to right.

(A) Since 2001, Incan ruins similar to Machu Picchu but without a visitor limit have disintegrated at a significantly greater rate than those on the Inca Trail.	*This sounds promising. The government's assumption was that the visitor limit helped prevent deterioration, so showing that other sites without limits did experience deterioration would make it more likely that the government's reasoning is valid. I'll definitely keep this one in.*	A̶
(B) Villages near Machu Picchu have experienced declines in income, as fewer tourists buy fewer craft goods and refreshments.	*This sounds bad for the villages, but it doesn't impact the specific claim about preventing deterioration along the trail.*	B̶
(C) Many of the funds from the sale of Inca Trail permits are used to hire guards for archaeological sites without permit programs.	*This sounds like a good use of funds, but it has nothing to do with whether the permit program really did help prevent deterioration. All this tells me is that maybe <u>other</u> sites are also better protected due to the guards.*	C̶
(D) Since 2001, tourist guides along the Inca Trail have received 50% to 100% increases in take-home pay.	*That's great for the guides. It doesn't impact the actual conclusion at all, though.*	D̶

5

| (E) The total number of tourists in Peru has risen substantially since 2001, even as the number of tourists hiking the Inca Trail has remained constant. | *This one's about the number of visitors again, so maybe it strengthens. Let's see. A lot more people are visiting Peru…oh, but the second part is what I was already told: visitors to the trail are limited. This doesn't add anything new that specifically affects the claim about deterioration along the trail.* | E |

8. Digital Video Recorders: The correct answer is **(C)**.

Did this one seem a little different from all of the others? We set a trap for you! This is a Find the Assumption question, not a Strengthen or a Weaken. We discussed Find the Assumption questions in the previous chapter (though we used a less common variant for the question wording, just to see whether you were paying attention). We did warn you at the beginning of this chapter to read the previous chapter first!

On the real test, you'll never have the luxury of knowing that the next question will be a certain type— so be prepared for *anything*.

Step 1: Identify the question.

| Which of the following is required in order for the advertising executive to claim that television commercials are less cost-effective today? | *The word "required" indicates that this is a Find the Assumption question.* | FA   A B C D E |

Step 2: Deconstruct the argument.

| Advertising Executive: More than 10 million households now own digital video recorders that can fast-forward over television commercials; | *This is just a fact.* | Exec: 10 mill + HH's = DVR |
| approximately 75% of these households fast-forward over at least one commercial per 30-minute program. | *Another fact. I don't think I need to write down the exact numerical details right now, but I'll note that there are numerical details with a # just to remind myself.* | 75% skip ads (#) |

MANHATTAN
PREP

Because television commercials are not as widely watched as they used to be, they are much less cost-effective today.	*This contains another premise and the conclusion. The premise: TV ads aren't as widely watched today. The conclusion: TV ads are much less cost-effective than they used to be.*	B/c ads now watched less, ads = less cost eff

Step 3: State the goal.

Okay, the advertising executive claims that TV ads are not as cost-effective specifically because people aren't watching them as much, and that is specifically because a lot of people fast-forward over at least some commercials. I want an answer that the author must believe to be true in order to draw that conclusion. What assumptions are being made?

Let's see. They're assuming that people really did watch TV commercials more before, but they don't provide any evidence of that. Maybe people used to tape programs on VCRs and then still fast-forward. They haven't actually told me what people used to do before these DVRs came along.

Step 4: Work from wrong to right.

(A) Product placement within television programs is a viable alternative to traditional television commercials.	*That's nice for the advertisers who want to make money, but this doesn't have to be true in order to claim that TV commercials are less cost-effective now.*	A̶
(B) The television programs preferred by consumers without digital video recorders are similar to those preferred by consumers with the devices.	*Hmm. The DVR thing was used as evidence to show how some people are skipping commercials. I don't think making a distinction about people with or without the DVRs really tells us anything. The conclusion is about commercials, not what programs people watch.*	B̶
(C) Prior to the advent of digital video recorders, very few television viewers switched channels or left the room when commercials began.	*That's interesting. People didn't used to change channels or leave the room, so maybe they really were watching more TV commercials. If I negate this answer, then it would say that people <u>did</u> switch channels or leave the room. If that were the case, then it'd be tough to claim that people watch fewer commercials nowadays. This choice looks good.*	C̲
(D) The cost-effectiveness of television advertising is based less upon how many people watch a particular commercial and more upon the appropriateness of the demographic.	*Hmm. They're saying that we should be using a different metric to evaluate cost-effectiveness, not how many people watch. Yeah, that sounds convincing. Wait! My goal is to find something that makes the argument more likely to be valid. If anything, this would weaken the argument: this is a Reverse Logic trap!*	D̶

| (E) Many companies find it difficult to determine the exact return on investment for television commercials. | *A lot of companies can't tell how much money they earn from people watching TV commercials. But maybe they can still tell something about the relative differences between a few years ago and now. Also, if this were actually true, if anything, the conclusion would be a little less valid, because that would mean we couldn't tell that the TV commercials are less cost-effective today.* | E |

A   B   Ⓒ   D   E

9. APR: The correct answer is **(E)**.

Step 1: Identify the question.

| Which of the following statements, if true, would most seriously undermine a plan to increase interest rates in order to spur profitable growth? | *The "undermine" and "if true" language indicates that this is a Weaken question. Further, the question stem tells me the conclusion: there's a plan to increase interest rates that will supposedly cause profits to grow.* | W   A B C D E
Ⓒ Plan: ↑ int rats → ↑ prof growth |

Step 2: Deconstruct the argument.

| CEO: Over the past several years, we have more than doubled our revenues but profits have steadily declined because an increasing number of customers have failed to pay their balances. | *Several facts here. Revenues have gone up but profits have gone down because the customers aren't paying what they owe.* | CEO: 2x rev but ↓ prof b/c cust not pay bills |
| In order to compensate for these higher default rates, we will increase the interest charged on outstanding balances from an annual percentage rate (APR) of 9.5% to an APR of 12%. | *Okay, here's the plan. They'll charge more interest to everyone to compensate for the people who aren't paying their bills.* | ↑ % int rate to comp |

MANHATTAN
PREP

This increase will be sufficient to compensate for the current rate of defaults and allow us to increase our profits.	*Hmm. They're claiming that 12% will be enough to compensate for the* <u>*current*</u> *rate of people who don't pay so that they can increase profits (which is the conclusion I already wrote down). They're assuming that the current rate isn't going to get worse in future.*	12% will be enough

Step 3: State the goal.

The company plans to charge higher interest rates in order to become profitable again. The evidence shows only that the higher interest rate will be sufficient for today's default rate; that could change over time.

This is a Weaken question so I need to find something that makes the CEO's conclusion less likely to be valid.

Step 4: Work from wrong to right.

(A) Many other companies have experienced a similar trend in their default rates.	*This doesn't address the company's plan to* <u>*fix*</u> *the problem: increasing the interest rate. This doesn't impact the conclusion at all.*	~~A~~
(B) The company's operating expenses are above the industry average and can be substantially reduced, thus increasing margins.	*Hmm. If the company does this, it could increase profits, which is the company's goal...but the conclusion is that the plan to increase interest rates will improve profits, and this choice doesn't address that plan. Plus, if anything, this choice makes it more likely that the company will increase profits, but I want to weaken the conclusion.*	~~B~~
(C) The increase in default rates was due to a rise in unemployment, but unemployment rates are expected to drop in the coming months.	*If unemployment caused people not to pay their bills, and fewer people are going to be unemployed, then maybe more will pay their bills? That would help the company, but I want something that will weaken the conclusion. And the conclusion is specifically about the plan. This choice doesn't address the specific plan about interest rates.*	~~C~~
(D) The proposed increase in the APR will, alone, more than double the company's profit margins.	*This supports the company's claim that increasing the interest rate will help raise profits. I want something that weakens that claim.*	~~D~~

5

| (E) An increase in the APR charged on credit card balances often results in higher rates of default. | *Okay, if they do increase the APR, then more people may stop paying their bills as a result! The conclusion specifically said that raising the APR would compensate for the "current rate of defaults," so if the rate goes up, then the company is less likely to increase its profits. This does weaken the conclusion.* | E̶ |

A̶   B̶   C̶   D̶   Ⓔ

10. Jupiter vs. Mars: The correct answer is **(D)**.

Step 1: Identify the question.

| Which of the following, if true, would most strengthen a contention by the government that the new project is a better use of its funds? | *The words "if true" and "strengthen a contention" indicate that this is a Strengthen question. Further, the question stem tells me the conclusion: the government claims that the new project is a better use of funds.* | S   A B C D E
Ⓒ Gov: new proj = better |

Step 2: Deconstruct the argument.

Scientists suspect that Europa, a moon orbiting Jupiter, may contain living organisms.	*There is a fact: scientists suspect something is true. I don't actually know whether it's true, though.*	Sci: Europa may have life
However, the government recently scrapped an unmanned science mission to Europa and replaced it with a project aimed at landing an astronaut on Mars.	*There was a project to send an unmanned mission to Europa, but that was replaced by another project to send a person to Mars. More facts.*	Ⓒ BUT gov replaced w/Mars proj
Polls show that the public is far more fascinated by space travel than by discovering life elsewhere in the universe.	*More facts—a survey showed that people like space travel more.*	Ppl like space travel more
Critics argue that the government's decision-making process places a greater emphasis on popularity than it does on the importance of scientific research.	*This is a counterconclusion. The critics say that the government is just paying attention to popularity of projects, but the question stem told me that the government claims that the new project is a better use of funds.*	Critics: gov cares more ab popularity

Step 3: State the goal.

There are two opposing points of view, the government and the critics. The government claims that the new project is a better use of funds. The critics claim that the government is paying more attention to popularity than to scientific research. The critics are assuming that, just because the public finds the Mars project more interesting, there aren't also good scientific reasons for replacing the Europa project with the Mars project.

I need to strengthen the government's claim. I need to be really careful that I don't mistakenly strengthen the critics' claim.

Step 4: Work from wrong to right.

(A) In the first year of the project, the government will spend 30% of its total budget on developing a space shuttle that can travel to Mars; that figure is expected to drop to 0% after five years.	*This doesn't give me any additional information as to why the Mars project is better than the Europa project. I don't know whether they'd be spending more or less on the Europa project, nor do I know what kind of good research they'll expect to get in return.*	A̶
(B) The government cannot be absolutely certain of the chances for success of either project.	*Was there anything in the argument that hinged on being absolutely certain of success? No. If they told me that the Mars project has a greater chance for success, that would be good—but knowing that, I <u>don't</u> know the chances for either project… that doesn't add anything.*	B̶
(C) Some scientists are convinced that a mission to Europa would add immeasurably to our understanding of the universe.	*This is a good reason to continue funding the mission to E. But that would support the critics, not the government. This is a trap.*	C̶
(D) A new telescope that has just become available to scientists promises to yield more information than the planned mission to Europa was designed to provide.	*Now they have a new telescope that they can use to get even more research than they would have if they sent an unmanned mission? That's a good reason to cancel the unmanned mission. If that's true, then pretty much any other decent project would be a better use of funds!*	D̰
(E) Most people feel that a shuttle to Mars is the next logical step in the development of a system that will allow humans to travel even further in the solar system.	*That's interesting, but it doesn't tell me anything <u>new</u> about why spending the money on the Mars project is better than spending money on the Europa project. I already know that people are more interested in space travel. This answer is a tangent that's trying to get me to think more about that and make me forget about the conclusion, which centered on a comparison of the two projects.*	E̶

A̶   B̶   C̶   Ⓓ   E̶

11. Deep-brain Stimulation: The correct answer is **(D)**.

Step 1: Identify the question.

Which of the following most logically completes the argument given below?	*The question appears before the argument, and the argument contains a blank at the end. Both of these things indicate that this is a Complete the Argument question.*	CA A B C D E

Step 2: Deconstruct the argument.

Deep-brain stimulation is a new technique for combating severe depression.	*Straight fact.*	Deep-brain stim combats depression
In a recent experiment, electrodes were implanted into the brains of six patients who had not responded to any currently approved treatment for depression.	*This tells me how it works and that they tested it on six people.*	Tested on 6 ppl
When an electrical current to the electrodes was switched on, four of the patients reported feeling a dramatic reduction in depressive symptoms.	*And four of the people got a lot better.*	4 better
The long-term prospects of the new treatment are not promising, however, because _____.	*Oh, but the author thinks the treatment's not really going to work long-term. Why?*	©BUT probably won't work, b/c …

Step 3: State the goal.

The author describes a new medical treatment but says it's probably not going to be good long-term; I need to find a reason why. So far, the only evidence given makes deep-brain stimulation sound promising, so I've got to find something that shows a flaw or weakness in the treatment.

Step 4: Work from wrong to right.

(A) other treatments for depression may also be effective	*This is probably true in the real world, but talking about other treatments doesn't explain why deep-brain stimulation won't be a good treatment long-term.*	A
(B) the other two patients reported only a slight reduction of depressive symptoms during the treatment	*When I saw the word "only," I was expecting them to say they had a bad result, but actually having even a slight reduction is better than nothing, especially for people who have tried other treatments that haven't worked. So, if anything, this is a plus for deep-brain stimulation. That's not what I want.*	B
(C) deep-brain stimulation relies on the expertise of highly skilled physicians	*I can believe this is true, but we would expect any major medical treatment to be performed by skilled physicians, so why would this make deep-brain stimulation not work long-term?*	C
(D) when the electrical current is interrupted, the effects of the treatment are reversed	*That's interesting. So, when the current is on, the symptoms go away, but when the current is off, the depression comes back. That means they'd have to be connected to some machine all the time—they couldn't just get a treatment once a week or once a month. That definitely makes the treatment less practical and promising. Unless choice (E) is better, this looks like the answer.*	D
(E) in a subsequent experiment, a one-hour treatment with the electrodes resulted in a sustained remission from depression in the four patients for six months	*This is almost the opposite of choice (D). If you get a one-hour treatment, then the symptoms go away for 6 months—that's great for deep-brain stimulation! This can't be the right answer.*	E

A   B   C   (D)   E

Chapter 6
of

Critical Reasoning

The Assumption Family: Evaluate the Argument and Find the Flaw

In This Chapter...

Evaluate the Argument Questions

The "Strengthen/Weaken" Strategy

Find the Flaw Questions

Chapter 6

The Assumption Family: Evaluate the Argument and Find the Flaw

In Chapters 4 and 5, you learned about the three major question types in the Assumption Family: Find the Assumption, Strengthen, and Weaken. If you haven't read those chapters yet, please do so before reading this chapter.

In addition, think about how much time you want to put into this chapter. Evaluate the Argument questions are somewhat uncommon—you'll most likely see just one or two. Find the Flaw questions are even rarer. If you have a very high Verbal goal (90th percentile or higher), then study these two question types. If your Verbal goal score is lower, consider guessing on Flaw questions. If you struggle with Evaluate questions, you might want to guess on those as well.

The Assumption lessons you learned earlier still apply to Evaluate and Flaw questions:

- Assumptions are something an author must believe to be true in order to draw his or her conclusion. These assumptions are not stated explicitly in the argument.

- All assumption arguments will contain a "core": a conclusion and the major premise or premises that lead to it.

- All assumption arguments will include at least one (and probably more than one) unstated assumption.

Evaluate and Flaw questions also hinge upon identifying an assumption, as you'd expect in the Assumption Family.

Evaluate the Argument Questions

For Evaluate questions, your first step is still to find an assumption, but you have to do a little more work to get to the answer. At heart, you are asked what additional information would help to determine whether the assumption is valid or invalid.

Most Evaluate question stems will contain one or more of the following:

- The word "evaluate" or a synonym
- The word "determine" or a synonym
- Language asking what would be "useful to know (or establish)" or "important to know"

For example, an Evaluate question stem might ask:

"Which of the following must be studied in order to evaluate the argument?"

"Which of the following would it be most useful to know in determining whether the mayor's plan is likely to be successful?"

Occasionally, an Evaluate question will use other wording, but the question will still get at the same overall idea—What information would help to evaluate the given argument? That information, if made available, would either strengthen or weaken that argument.

The "Strengthen/Weaken" Strategy

Evaluate answer choices will often be in the form of a question or in the form of "whether" a certain thing is one way or the other. For example, say you're asked to evaluate this argument:

In order to increase its profits, MillCo plans to reduce costs by laying off any nonessential employees.

Hmm. According to the argument:

MillCo will lay off nonessential employees → reduce costs → increase profits

Does that sound like a good plan? What is MillCo assuming in claiming that laying off nonessential employees will result in increased profits?

Profits are a measure of revenues minus costs. So, for one thing, MillCo is assuming that revenues won't drop a lot as a result of these layoffs. If revenues dropped as much as or more than the expected cost savings, then MillCo's profits wouldn't increase.

A correct answer to the Evaluate question about the argument above might read:

> Whether revenues will be affected adversely enough to threaten MillCo's profit structure.

This "whether" does something very interesting to the argument. Imagine that you could find out whether revenues will be affected adversely. The argument would be strengthened one way and weakened the other. Take a look:

> Yes, the plan *will* affect MillCo's revenues adversely enough to threaten profits. In this case, the plan to increase profits is less likely to work, so the argument is weakened.

> No, the plan *won't* affect MillCo's revenues adversely enough to threaten profits. In this case, the plan to increase profits is a little more likely to work, so the argument is strengthened

This answer choice, then, actually *tests* the assumption: if it goes one way, the argument is strengthened, and if it goes the other way, the argument is weakened.

The correct answer will be structured in such a way that these two possible "paths" exist, one strengthening and one weakening the argument.

The incorrect answers will be presented in a similar format, but won't actually test the strength of the argument. What if you had the following answer choice?

> Whether MillCo might reduce its costs more by eliminating some health insurance benefits for the remaining employees

Evaluate the two paths:

> Yes, MillCo can reduce costs more by eliminating some health benefits. How will this affect the given plan to lay off employees? Technically, this doesn't impact whether laying off certain employees will improve profits. It is true that reducing costs could help to increase profits, but the argument specifies that MillCo will reduce costs specifically by laying off nonessential employees. Whether the company could also reduce costs in some other way has no bearing on this specific argument.

> No, MillCo cannot reduce costs more by eliminating some health benefits. This certainly doesn't strengthen the argument. It doesn't weaken the argument either, though, since the argument hinges on laying off employees. This path does nothing to the argument.

This incorrect answer choice is trying to distract you by offering a different way to increase profits, but you aren't asked to find alternative ways to increase profits. You're asked to evaluate whether the *existing argument* involving this particular path to profits is valid. The answer doesn't provide a strengthen/weaken pair here, so the choice cannot be the right answer.

On Evaluate questions, you're going to do what you do on all Assumption Family questions:

1. Find the core (conclusion plus major premises).
2. Take note of any assumptions that jump out at you.

Then you're going to look for an answer that addresses an assumption (maybe one that you've noticed, but not necessarily!). The correct answer should offer two different "paths," one that would make the argument stronger and one that would make the argument weaker.

Try a full example; set your timer for two minutes. If you get stuck, pick an answer before you read the explanation. During the real test, you'll have to pick an answer in order to move on, so practice letting go and guessing.

Food allergies account for more than 30,000 emergency room visits each year. Often, victims of these episodes are completely unaware of their allergies until they experience a major reaction. Studies show that 90% of food allergy reactions are caused by only eight distinct foods. For this reason, individuals should sample a minuscule portion of each of these foods to determine whether a particular food allergy is present.

Which of the following must be studied in order to evaluate the recommendation made in the argument?

(A) The percentage of allergy victims who were not aware of the allergy before a major episode
(B) The percentage of the population that is at risk for allergic reactions
(C) Whether some of the eight foods are common ingredients used in cooking
(D) Whether an allergy to one type of food makes someone more likely to be allergic to other types of food
(E) Whether ingesting a very small amount of an allergen is sufficient to provoke an allergic reaction in a susceptible individual

Step 1: Identify the question.

Which of the following must be studied in order to evaluate the recommendation made in the argument?	*The words "must be studied" and "evaluate" indicate that this is an Evaluate question.*	Ev A B C D E

6

Step 2: Deconstruct the argument.

Food allergies account for more than 30,000 emergency room visits each year.	*This is a fact.*	Food allerg → 30k ER/yr
Often, victims of these episodes are completely unaware of their allergies until they experience a major reaction.	*Fact but more fuzzy. A lot of people don't know they're allergic till they have a major reaction.*	Ppl unaware till have rxn
Studies show that 90% of food allergy reactions are caused by only eight distinct foods.	*More facts! That's interesting. Only eight foods cause most allergic reactions.*	only 8 foods → 90% rxns
For this reason, individuals should sample a minuscule portion of each of these foods to determine whether a particular food allergy is present.	*This is the conclusion. The author's saying we should all try a tiny bit of these eight foods to see what happens. That assumes that we'll actually have a reaction from a tiny amount. It also assumes we won't die from just a tiny amount (if we are allergic).*	©Ppl shld try tiny bit of 8 foods to test

Step 3: State the goal.

This is an Evaluate question, so I need to find an answer that will help to determine whether or not the conclusion is likely to be valid. The correct answer will have "two paths": one path will make the conclusion a little more likely to be valid and the other will make the conclusion a little less likely to be valid.

In this case, the author recommends that we all try tiny bits of these eight foods to see whether we're allergic. The author's assuming that we can tell whether we're allergic from trying just a tiny bit. The author is also assuming that these micro-tests won't endanger us either!

6

Step 4: Work from wrong to right.

(A) The percentage of allergy victims who were not aware of the allergy before a major episode	*The argument said that victims "often" aren't aware of the allergy beforehand. If I knew that 90% weren't aware, that would go along with what the argument already says. If I knew that 50% weren't aware…hmm, that wouldn't change the argument. In general, knowing the exact percentage doesn't change anything.*	A̶
(B) The percentage of the population that is at risk for allergic reactions	*If a really high percentage is at risk for allergies, then it's probably important to figure out whether people are allergic…but that doesn't mean that the specific recommendation in the conclusion here is a good one or bad one. Also, this answer choice doesn't specifically limit itself to food allergies; it mentions all allergies in general.*	B̶
(C) Whether some of the eight foods are common ingredients used in cooking	*If yes, then many people may have already tried small amounts of these foods. That doesn't actually tell me, though, whether the recommendation is a good one. If no, then it doesn't affect the conclusion at all—I still don't know whether it's a good recommendation.*	C̶
(D) Whether an allergy to one type of food makes someone more likely to be allergic to other types of food	*If yes or if no, I'd still want to test people to see whether they're allergic to anything. This choice doesn't have "two paths" that lead to alternate outcomes.*	D̶
(E) Whether ingesting a very small amount of an allergen is sufficient to provoke an allergic reaction in a susceptible individual	*This is one of the things I said! If yes, then the author's plan will work: people will be able to try small amounts and determine whether they're allergic. If no, then the author's plan is not a good one: trying small amounts won't actually help you tell whether you're allergic.*	E̲

A̶   B̶   C̶   D̶   Ⓔ

Common Trap Answers

The wrong answers are very tricky. How do the test writers get you to pick wrong answers on Evaluate questions?

No Tie to the Argument

Answer (C) presented something that seemed like it would matter: maybe lots of people have already tried the eight foods. What does that mean for the recommendation? Maybe some people have already had reactions to some foods. But some people might have tried only six of the eight, so maybe they should still try the other two. Or maybe … You could speculate endlessly, but all paths lead to the same place: this choice doesn't impact whether the specific recommendation made is good or bad.

Irrelevant Distinction or Comparison

You saw this trap for the first time in the Find the Assumption chapter. In the above problem, answer (D) does discuss something mentioned by the argument—allergies—but tries to talk about whether someone might have more than one allergy; this is not at issue in the argument. The argument only distinguishes those with allergies and those without.

6

Find the Flaw Questions

Find the Flaw questions are the least common of the five Assumption Family question types. The question stems will almost always contain some form of the word "flaw," but be careful: Weaken the Argument questions also might contain the word "flaw" in the question stem.

Here's how to tell the difference. Weaken questions will also contain "if true" language. Flaw questions will *not* contain this language. Take a look at the chart below:

Flaw	Weaken
Look for this first:	
Contains the word "flaw" but NOT "if true" language.	Contains the word "flaw" AND the words "if true" (or an equivalent synonym).
If you're still not sure, try this:	
Answer choices are a bit more abstract, similar to but not as abstract as Structure Family questions.	Answer choices represent a new piece of information (as described in the discussion of the Weaken question type).
Example	
Which of the following indicates a *flaw* in the reasoning above?	Which of the following, *if true*, would indicate a *flaw* in the teacher's plan?

On occasion, a Flaw question may contain a synonym of the word "flaw," such as "vulnerable to criticism."

As with the other Assumption Family questions, Find the Flaw questions will contain an argument core, and it's great if you notice assumptions that the author makes. The correct answer, though, will be essentially the opposite of the correct answer on a Find the Assumption question. On Find the Assumption, you pick an answer that articulates an assumption that is necessary to the argument. On Flaw questions, by contrast, you are looking for wording that indicates why it is *flawed* thinking to believe that this assumption is true.

For example:

> Pierre was recovering from the flu when he visited Shelley last week, and now Shelley is showing signs of the flu. If Pierre had waited until he was no longer contagious, Shelley would not have become ill.

The author is assuming that Pierre was definitely the one to infect Shelley. The author is also assuming that there is no other way Shelley could have gotten sick. Perhaps it is flu season, and many people with whom Shelley came in contact had the flu!

The correct answer might be something like:

> The author fails to consider that there are alternate paths by which Shelley could have become infected.

Contrast that language with the assumption itself: the author assumes that only Pierre could have infected Shelley. If that's true, then that piece of information at least partially fixes the author's argument. When you take the same information, though, and flip it around into a flaw, you harm the author's argument:

Pierre was recovering from the flu when he visited Shelley last week, and now Shelley is showing signs of the flu. If Pierre had waited until he was no longer contagious, Shelley would not have become ill.	
Assumption	*Flaw*
Only Pierre could have infected Shelley.	The author fails to consider that there are alternate paths by which Shelley could have become infected.
The argument is made stronger.	*The argument is made weaker.*

In sum, think of Flaw questions as the "reverse" of Assumption questions. The answer still hinges on an assumption, but the correct answer will word that assumption in a way that hurts the argument.

In addition, the answer choice language may be a bit more abstract than the answer choices on other Assumption Family questions. Often, the answer choices will talk about what the author "fails to consider (or establish)," "does not specify (or identify)," or something along those lines.

Try this full example:

> Environmentalist: Bando Inc.'s manufacturing process releases pollution into the atmosphere. In order to convince the company to change processes, we will organize a boycott of the product that represents its highest sales volume, light bulbs. Because Bando sells more light bulbs than any other product, a boycott of light bulbs will cause the most damage to the company's profits.
>
> The environmentalist's reasoning is flawed because it fails to

(A) allow for the possibility that Bando may not want to change its manufacturing process

(B) supply information about other possible ways for Bando to reduce pollution

(C) consider that the relative sales volumes of a company's products are not necessarily proportional to profits

(D) identify any alternate methods by which to convince Bando to change its manufacturing process

(E) consider that a boycott may take too long to achieve its purpose

Step 1: Identify the question.

The environmentalist's reasoning is flawed because it fails to	*The word "flawed" indicates that this is either a Flaw or a Weaken question. "If true" does not appear, so this is a Flaw question. I'll write down "Fl" on my scrap paper.*	Fl A B C D E

Step 2: Deconstruct the argument.

Environmentalist: Bando Inc.'s manufacturing process releases pollution into the atmosphere.	*This is a fact (assume the environmentalist is telling the truth).*	Environ-ist: manuf → atmo pollutn
In order to convince the company to change processes, we will organize a boycott of the product that represents its highest sales volume, light bulbs.	*Okay, here's a plan, so it's likely a conclusion. They think if they boycott something, this company might change its manufacturing process. So they're going to boycott light bulbs because Bando sells more light bulbs than anything else.*	boyc bulbs (↑ sales) → so company Δ manuf
Because Bando sells more light bulbs than any other product, a boycott of light bulbs will cause the most damage to the company's profits.	*Another claim. Because they sell more light bulbs than anything else, the environmentalist figures that a boycott of light bulbs will do the most damage to profits. Profits? How profitable are the light bulbs?* *Okay, the conclusion was the previous sentence, because all of this is designed to convince Bando to change its manufacturing process.*	Bando sells ↑ bulbs → boyc → ↑ damage to prof

Step 3: State the goal.

The environmentalist doesn't like that Bando pollutes. Bando sells more light bulbs than any other product, so the environmentalist wants to boycott those bulbs to do the most damage to Bando's profits (according to this environmentalist, anyway), and then the hope is that this will all cause the company to change its manufacturing process.

I need to find an answer that will articulate a flaw in that reasoning. I've already thought of one. The environmentalist is assuming that just because Bando sells more light bulbs than anything else, the company is also earning the most profits from those products. But there's no evidence to support that. Also, consumers might not actually agree to boycott Bando.

MANHATTAN
PREP

Step 4: Work from wrong to right.

(A) allow for the possibility that Bando may not want to change its manufacturing process	*If anything, it could be argued that the environmentalist is already assuming the company will not want to change—that's why the environmentalist thinks he or she has to organize a boycott to change the company's mind!*	A
(B) does not supply information about other possible ways for Bando to reduce pollution	*In the real world, I agree that environmentalist's should explore all possible ways…but the question asks me to find a flaw in this particular plan about the boycott. This doesn't apply to that plan.*	B
(C) consider that the relative sales volumes of a company's products are not necessarily proportional to profits	*This sounds kind of like what I said before. It's a little abstract, so I'm not sure I fully understand all of it, but it does say that sales aren't necessarily proportional to profits. I'll keep this one in.*	C
(D) identify any alternative methods by which to convince Bando to change its manufacturing process	*This is like choice (B). It'd be good in general for the environmentalist to do this…but this doesn't help me figure out a flaw in the boycott plan specifically.*	D
(E) consider that a boycott may take too long to achieve its purpose	*I think what really matters is whether the plan is going to work at all, not how long it takes. The argument doesn't have any requirements about how long it will take to get Bando to change its process.*	E

A   B   (C)   D   E

Common Trap Answers

Irrelevant Distinction or Comparison

This trap discusses alternative plans or paths when you were asked to comment on the given plan, similar to answers (B) and (D) in the above example. A choice can also bring up a detail or distinction that does not actually affect the argument, similar to choice (E) in the above problem

Flaw questions may also occasionally use **Reverse Logic**, similar to answer choice (A) in the above example.

Cheat Sheets

Evaluate Cheat Sheet

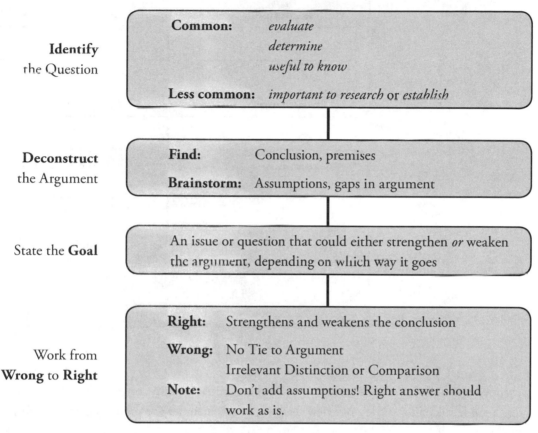

Identify the Question

Common:	*evaluate*
	determine
	useful to know
Less common:	*important to research* or *establish*

Deconstruct the Argument

| **Find:** | Conclusion, premises |
| **Brainstorm:** | Assumptions, gaps in argument |

State the **Goal**

An issue or question that could either strengthen *or* weaken the argument, depending on which way it goes

Work from **Wrong** to **Right**

Right:	Strengthens and weakens the conclusion
Wrong:	No Tie to Argument
	Irrelevant Distinction or Comparison
Note:	Don't add assumptions! Right answer should work as is.

Photocopy this page and keep it with the review sheets you're creating as you study. Better yet, use this page as a guide to create your own review sheet—you'll remember the material better if you write it down yourself.

Flaw Cheat Sheet

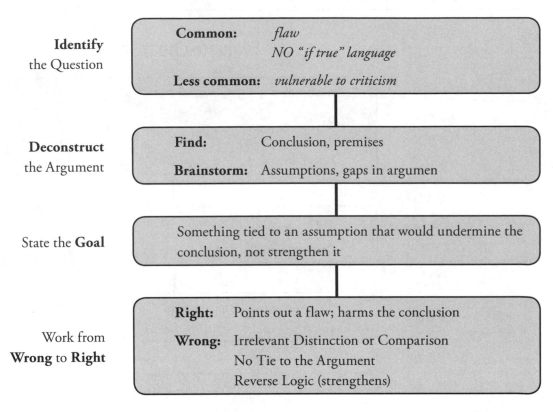

Identify
the Question

Common:	*flaw*
	NO "if true" language
Less common:	*vulnerable to criticism*

Deconstruct
the Argument

Find:	Conclusion, premises
Brainstorm:	Assumptions, gaps in argumen

State the **Goal**

Something tied to an assumption that would undermine the conclusion, not strengthen it

Work from
Wrong to **Right**

Right:	Points out a flaw; harms the conclusion
Wrong:	Irrelevant Distinction or Comparison
	No Tie to the Argument
	Reverse Logic (strengthens)

Photocopy this page and keep it with the review sheets you're creating as you study. Better yet, use this page as a guide to create your own review sheet—you'll remember the material better if you write it down yourself.

Problem Set

Answer each question using the four-step CR process. Check your answer after each question. As you improve, consider timing yourself; critical reasoning questions need to be completed in an average of two minutes.

1. *Tuition*

    Recently, the tuition at most elite private colleges has been rising faster than inflation. Even before these increases, many low- and middle-income families were unable to afford the full tuition costs for their children at these institutions of higher learning. With the new tuition increases, these colleges will soon cater solely to students with affluent family backgrounds.

    Which of the following would it be most useful to determine in order to evaluate the argument?

    (A) Whether students from affluent families are more likely to prefer public or private colleges

    (B) Whether students from low- and middle-income families are qualified to attend elite private colleges

    (C) Whether low-income families are less likely to be able to afford tuition costs than middle-income families

    (D) Whether tuition costs at elite public colleges have also been rising faster than inflation

    (E) Whether grants or scholarships are earmarked for students from economically disadvantaged families

2. *Charity*

    Studies show that impoverished families give away a larger percentage of their income in charitable donations than do wealthy families. As a result, fundraising consultants recommend that charities direct their marketing efforts toward individuals and families from lower socioeconomic classes in order to maximize the dollar value of incoming donations.

    Which of the following best explains why the consultants' reasoning is flawed?

    (A) Marketing efforts are only one way to solicit charitable donations.

    (B) Not all impoverished families donate to charity.

    (C) Some charitable marketing efforts are so expensive that the resulting donations fail to cover the costs of the marketing campaign.

    (D) Percentage of income is not necessarily indicative of absolute dollar value.

    (E) People are more likely to donate to the same causes to which their friends donate.

3. *CostMart*

Editorial: In order to preserve the health of its local economy, Metropolis should not permit a CostMart warehouse department store to open within city limits. It has been demonstrated that when CostMart opens a warehouse department store within a city, the bankruptcy rate of local retailers increases in that city by 20% over the next several years.

Which of the following questions would be most useful for evaluating the conclusion of the editorial?

(A) Does the bankruptcy rate of local retailers in a city generally stabilize several years after a CostMart warehouse department store opens?

(B) Do most residents of Metropolis currently do almost all of their shopping at stores within the city limits of Metropolis?

(C) Have other cities that have permitted CostMart warehouse department stores within city limits experienced any economic benefits as a result?

(D) Is the bankruptcy rate for local retailers in Metropolis higher than in the average city that has permitted a CostMart warehouse department store within city limits?

(E) Does CostMart plan to hire employees exclusively from within Metropolis for the proposed warehouse department store?

4. *Five-Step Process*

Manager: The new manufacturing process should save us time overall, even though the first step of the five-step process will take twice as long as it does under the old process. Under the new process, far fewer of the components will be found defective, and the sole purpose of steps two and three under the old process is to weed out defective components. As a result, we should be able to eliminate two of the five steps in the existing manufacturing process.

Which of the following would be most useful in evaluating the claim made in the argument?

(A) Whether factory workers will require training in order to use the new manufacturing process

(B) Whether the new process is likely to introduce deficiencies or imperfections that must be corrected

(C) Whether defective components can be fixed or must be thrown out

(D) Whether a third manufacturing process would save even more time than both the old and new manufacturing processes

(E) Whether saving time with the new manufacturing process will ultimately lead to cost savings for the company

MANHATTAN
PREP

5. *Ethanol*

Ethanol, a fuel derived from corn, can be used alone to power cars or along with gasoline to reduce the amount of gas consumed. Unlike gasoline, ethanol is easily renewable since it is primarily converted from the sun's energy. Moreover, compared with conventional gasoline, pure ethanol is a cleaner-burning fuel. To save energy and reduce pollution, many individuals advocate the increased usage of ethanol as a primary fuel source in conjunction with or in place of gasoline.

In evaluating the recommendation to increase the use of ethanol, it would be important to research all of the following EXCEPT:

(A) Whether the energy required to grow and process corn used as fuel is greater than the amount of energy ultimately produced

(B) Whether more energy is saved when using ethanol in conjunction with or in place of gasoline

(C) Whether ethanol is as efficient a fuel as gasoline

(D) Whether it is possible to produce more ethanol than is currently produced

(E) Whether the process of growing corn for fuel would result in as much pollution as does the production of conventional gasoline

6

Solutions

1. Tuition: The correct answer is (**E**).

Step 1: Identify the question.

Which of the following would it be most useful to determine in order to evaluate the argument?	*Contains the words "evaluate" and "useful to determine"—this is an Evaluate question.*	Ev A B C D E

Step 2: Deconstruct the argument.

Recently, the tuition at most elite private colleges has been rising faster than inflation.	*Fact: tuition at this specific type of school has been going up even faster than inflation.*	↑ priv coll tuit > infl
Even before these increases, many low- and middle-income families were unable to afford the full tuition costs for their children at these institutions of higher learning.	*And many people without much money already couldn't afford these schools, even before the tuition went up. Another fact.*	B4: mid inc fams can't afford
With the new tuition increases, these colleges will soon cater solely to students with affluent family backgrounds.	*This must be the conclusion because the other two were facts, and this is a prediction about the future. Basically, they're saying that only wealthy students are going to be able to afford these schools now.*	Ⓒ priv coll will have only rich students

Step 3: State the goal.

This is an Evaluate question, so I need to find an answer that will help to determine whether or not the conclusion is likely to be valid. The correct answer will have "two paths": one path will make the conclusion a little more likely to be valid, and the other will make the conclusion a little less likely to be valid.

The conclusion is that <u>only</u> wealthy students are going to be able to go to these elite private colleges. What is the author assuming? Absolutely none of the low- or middle-income students can afford these schools. Non-wealthy students aren't going to be taking out loans, or working their way through school, or finding some other way to cover the tuition costs.

Step 4: Work from wrong to right.

(A) Whether students from affluent families are more likely to prefer public or private colleges	*If affluent students prefer public colleges, that doesn't change the fact that the private colleges charge a lot of money and poorer students can't afford them. If affluent students prefer private colleges, that also doesn't change the same fact.*	A
(B) Whether students from low- and middle-income families are qualified to attend elite private colleges	*If these students are not qualified to attend the elite private colleges, that doesn't change anything about the tuition issue. If these students are qualified, that also doesn't change the tuition issue (though it makes it seem unfair that the colleges charge so much money!).*	B
(C) Whether low-income families are less likely to be able to afford tuition costs than middle-income families	*This answer makes a distinction between low- and middle-income families, but the argument doesn't distinguish between these two groups—it combines them. Logically, it would make sense that the less money a family has, the less likely it could afford the tuition… but this doesn't change anything about the basic argument that low- and middle-income families can't afford the tuition.*	C̶
(D) Whether tuition costs at elite public colleges have also been rising faster than inflation	*If they have, then maybe that means lower-income students can't afford those schools either…but it might not mean anything, because perhaps the public schools have lower tuition fees in the first place. If rates have not been rising as fast at public colleges…that doesn't affect the argument's conclusion at all.*	D̶
(E) Whether grants or scholarships are earmarked for students from economically disadvantaged families	*If there are grants and scholarships for lower-income students, then perhaps they can afford to attend these colleges—this hurts the argument's conclusion. If there are not grants and scholarships for these students, then the argument's conclusion is more likely to be true: these students won't be able to afford these colleges. The "two paths" on this answer do lead to strengthening the conclusion on one hand and weakening it on the other.*	Ḛ

2. Charity: The correct answer is **(D)**.

Step 1: Identify the question.

Which of the following best explains why the consultants' reasoning is flawed?	The word "flawed" indicates that this is either a Flaw or Weaken question. The lack of the words "if true" (or an equivalent) means that this is a Flaw question.	F A B C D E

Step 2: Deconstruct the argument.

Studies show that impoverished families give away a larger percentage of their income in charitable donations than do wealthy families.	This is a fact. It's impressive that the poor donate anything, but if they do donate anything, then this fact makes sense because donating $100 is a much greater percentage of your income if you don't have much income.	Poor donate > % inc than rich
As a result, fundraising consultants recommend that charities direct their marketing efforts toward individuals and families from lower socioeconomic classes in order to maximize the dollar value of incoming donations.	This is the conclusion. Based on the percentage info, the consultants are saying that the charities should focus on lower income people…but the consultants are assuming that "greater percentage" equals more money. A very rich person might donate $10 million, a small percentage of income but a very large sum.	©Consultants: to get most $, char shld focus on ↓ inc ppl

Step 3: State the goal.

For Flaw questions, it's important to find the conclusion and brainstorm any assumptions, if I can. I need to find an answer that hurts the argument or shows why the argument is not a good argument.

In this case, the fundraising consultants are recommending that the charities target lower income families in order to maximize the number of dollars they get in donations. I've identified one potential assumption: the consultants assume that donating a greater percentage of income also means donating a greater dollar amount collectively. If that's not actually the case, then that's a flaw.

Step 4: Work from wrong to right.

(A) Marketing efforts are only one way to solicit charitable donations.	*This might be true, but it just indicates that there might be other ways, in addition to marketing efforts, to raise money. That doesn't affect the consultants' recommendation to target lower-income families in particular.*	A̶
(B) Not all impoverished families donate to charity.	*I'm sure this is true, but how does it affect the conclusion? It doesn't. The argument never claims that ALL impoverished families donate to charity—only that, in general, they donate a larger percentage of income to charity.*	B̶
(C) Some charitable marketing efforts are so expensive that the resulting donations fail to cover the costs of the marketing campaign.	*Oh, maybe this is it. If you spend more on the marketing than you make from donations, that can't be a very successful marketing campaign. What was the conclusion again? Oh, wait, "to maximize the dollar value of donations." Whether the marketing covered costs isn't part of the conclusion—it just depended on how much money they get in donations. Tricky, but not correct.*	C̶
(D) Percentage of income is not necessarily indicative of absolute dollar value.	*This is what I was saying before about the really rich person donating $10 million! You can have a bunch of low-income people give 10% of their income and one billionaire give 9% of her income…and the billionaire could be giving more in terms of absolute dollars. This indicates the flawed assumption made by the fundraising consultants.*	D
(E) People are more likely to donate to the same causes to which their friends donate.	*I can believe that this is true, but the argument doesn't address which causes people choose for charity. Rather, the argument talks about amount of money donated.*	E̶

A̶   B̶   C̶   E̶

6

3. CostMart: The correct answer is **(C)**.

Step 1: Identify the question.

Which of the following questions would be most useful for evaluating the conclusion of the editorial?	*The language "most useful" and "evaluating" indicates that this is an Evaluate question.*	Ev A B C D E

Step 2: Deconstruct the argument.

Editorial: In order to preserve the health of its local economy, Metropolis should not permit a CostMart warehouse department store to open within city limits.	*"In order to" means that something is going to cause this. Okay, the author is saying that Metropolis shouldn't let CostMart into the city so that Metropolis can preserve the health of the local economy. That's causation and kind of sounds like a conclusion.*	© Metrop shld ban Cost-Mart in city → help loc econ
It has been demonstrated that when CostMart opens a warehouse department store within a city, the bankruptcy rate of local retailers increases in that city by 20% over the next several years.	*There's a bad economic outcome for local retailers when a new Cost-Mart store opens. So certainly this is evidence that supports the author's claim that preventing CostMart from opening a store will preserve the local economy. This is a premise, so the previous sentence was the conclusion.*	new store → bnkrpt locals ↑ 20%
(Think about assumptions.)	*Are there any good economic results when CostMart opens a store? Maybe there are some bad and good results…and maybe the good results could outweigh the bad.*	[any good results?]

Step 3: State the goal.

I need to find an answer that will have two possible paths—one way will strengthen the author's claim, and the other way will weaken it. Could there be some good economic results for the local economy from a new CostMart?

Step 4: Work from wrong to right.

(A) Does the bankruptcy rate of local retailers in a city generally stabilize several years after a CostMart warehouse department store opens?	*If yes, then the bad result wouldn't continue to happen over time…but it would still happen in the first place. If no, then the bad result would keep happening over time. Either way, there is a bad result for at least a few years, so both "paths" strengthen the author's conclusion.*	A̶
(B) Do most residents of Metropolis currently do almost all of their shopping at stores within the city limits of Metropolis?	*If yes, then…I'm not sure what this has to do with the conclusion. If some stores go out of business, then people will have to switch stores? Okay, but that doesn't impact the city's overall economic situation—either there are local retailers or there's the CostMart store in the city (or both).*	B̶
(C) Have other cities that have permitted CostMart warehouse department stores within city limits experienced any economic benefits as a result?	*If yes, then that would be a reason to let CostMart open a store (because economic benefits would help to "preserve the health of the local economy"); that weakens the author's argument. If no, then there would seem to be no benefits to a CostMart store, and this strengthens the author's claim. This one is looking pretty good.*	C̲
(D) Is the bankruptcy rate for local retailers in Metropolis higher than in the average city that has permitted a CostMart warehouse department store within city limits?	*If yes, then…would that make local stores even more likely to go out of business if CostMart shows up? I'm not sure—I don't know why they're going out of business now. This doesn't seem to affect the conclusion one way or the other.*	D̶
(E) Does CostMart plan to hire employees exclusively from within Metropolis for the proposed warehouse department store?	*This one could be good, too. If yes, then that would be an economic benefit—jobs are good! If no, then…hmm…it's not bad necessarily but it's not good either, so I'll have to be sure.*	E̲
Compare (C) and (E).	*Wait. For (E), if some stores are going out of business, then people will lose jobs. In order for this to be a benefit, the new jobs added would have to be more than the jobs that are lost. Who knows whether that will happen? So there's no definite benefit given in (E), but there is in (C). Tricky.*	C̲ E̶

A̶ B̶ Ⓒ D̶ E̲

6

4. Five-Step Process: The correct answer is **(B)**.

Step 1: Identify the question.

Which of the following would be most useful in evaluating the claim made in the argument?	*The language "most useful in evaluating" indicates that this is an Evaluate question.*	Ev A B C D E

Step 2: Deconstruct the argument.

Manager: The new manufacturing process should save us time overall, even though the first step of the five-step process will take twice as long as it does under the old process.	*This is a claim. It could be the conclusion—I'll have to keep reading to tell.*	Mgr: New process faster though step 1 = 2x longer
Under the new process, far fewer of the components will be found defective, and the sole purpose of steps two and three under the old process is to weed out defective components.	*This seems to be a combo of a claim and a fact, but both are supporting the first sentence.*	Fewer bad parts Old process steps 2 + 3 for bad parts
As a result, we should be able to eliminate two of the five steps in the existing manufacturing process.	*Yes, the first sentence was the conclusion. If the other things are all true, then maybe the new manufacturing process will be faster than the old one.*	so can elim

Step 3: State the goal.

This is an Evaluate question, so I need to find an answer that will help to determine whether or not the conclusion is likely to be valid. The correct answer will have "two paths": one path will make the conclusion a little more likely to be valid, and the other will make the conclusion a little less likely to be valid.

The manager is claiming that the new process will be faster than the old process. Although the first step will take twice as long under the new process, the manager claims they "should" be able to drop the second and third steps. If dropping the second and third steps saves even more time than is lost during the first step, then the manager might be right…but the manager is assuming that these other steps will save a lot more time.

Step 4: Work from wrong to right.

(A) Whether factory workers will require training in order to use the new manufacturing process	*If they do…that may or may not affect how much time the process takes. If they don't, I still don't know anything more about how much time the new process is going to take versus the old process.*	A̶
(B) Whether the new process is likely to introduce deficiencies or imperfections that must be corrected	*If the new process also introduces problems that then need to be fixed, then perhaps they can't drop steps two and three, or perhaps they have to introduce other new steps to fix the deficiencies…either of which would add time to the new process, making it less likely that the new process will save time. If the new process does not introduce new imperfections that need to be fixed, then that increases the likelihood that the new process will save time.*	B̰
(C) Whether defective components can be fixed or must be thrown out	*If defective components can be fixed, that would add time to the process. If defective components must be thrown out, that would also add manufacturing time, because they would have to make even more. This doesn't give me two different paths, one of which helps the conclusion and one of which hurts the conclusion.*	C̶
(D) Whether a third manufacturing process would save even more time than both the old and new manufacturing processes	*The conclusion focuses on whether the new process is faster than the old process. Introducing a third, different process tells me nothing about the first two processes or how long they are.*	D̶
(E) Whether saving time with the new manufacturing process will ultimately lead to cost savings for the company	*The argument does not address anything about cost savings—the focus of the argument's conclusion is solely about saving time. Whether the company ultimately saves money does not tell me whether they'll save time.*	E̶

A̶   Ⓑ   C̶   D̶   E̶

5. Ethanol: The correct answer is (B).

Step 1: Identify the question.

In evaluating the recommendation to increase the use of ethanol, it would be important to research all of the following EXCEPT:	*The word "evaluating" (the conclusion) tells me that this is an Evaluate question. It's also an EXCEPT question. The four wrong ones WILL be important to evaluate; the correct answer will NOT be important to evaluate. The conclusion will have something to do with using ethanol.*	Ev Ex A B C D E

Step 2: Deconstruct the argument.

Ethanol, a fuel derived from corn, can be used alone to power cars or along with gasoline to reduce the amount of gas consumed.	*All facts. Ethanol is a kind of fuel, and it can be used in cars, either alone or with gas.*	Eth = fuel, alone or w/gas ↓ use of gas
Unlike gasoline, ethanol is easily renewable since it is primarily converted from the sun's energy.	*Interesting. It's easier to get more ethanol than more gasoline.*	Renewable
Moreover, compared with conventional gasoline, pure ethanol is a cleaner-burning fuel.	*And ethanol is "cleaner burning." Sounds pretty good so far.*	Clean burn
To save energy and reduce pollution, many individuals advocate the increased usage of ethanol as a primary fuel source in conjunction with or in place of gasoline.	*Conclusion! Many people think that using ethanol will save energy and reduce pollution.* (Note: NRG is an abbreviation for energy.)	Ⓒ Use more eth to save NRG, red pollut

6

Step 3: State the goal.

Ethanol as a fuel has various good qualities, so many people say we should use it and we'll save energy and reduce pollution.

On regular Evaluate questions, I try to find an answer that will tell me <u>whether</u> the conclusion is more or less valid. The answer can take me down two "paths," one of which will make the conclusion better and the other of which will make it worse. On this EXCEPT question, all four wrong answers will work this way. I'm looking for the "odd one out" that does NOT take me down two paths.

Step 4: Work from wrong to right.

(A) Whether the energy required to grow and process corn used as fuel is greater than the amount of energy ultimately produced	*The conclusion specifically claims that we'll <u>save</u> energy. If the amount of energy to produce ethanol is MORE than the amount of energy produced, then we aren't saving energy. If the amount of energy to produce ethanol is LESS than the amount of energy produced, then we are saving energy. This answer gives me "two paths" so it's wrong (since I want the EXCEPT answer).*	A̶
(B) Whether more energy is saved when using ethanol in conjunction with or in place of gasoline	*This answer choice uses many of the same words as the conclusion. But that's a trap! The conclusion makes no distinction between these two methods of using ethanol; it just recommends in general that we do use ethanol. If more energy is saved using ethanol in conjunction with gasoline, then the conclusion holds. If more energy is saved using ethanol in place of gasoline, then the conclusion holds. Either way, it's the same thing! There aren't "two paths" here. I'll keep this one.*	B̰
(C) Whether ethanol is as efficient a fuel as gasoline	*If ethanol is as efficient as or more efficient than gasoline, then we could use less ethanol to get the same amount of power. That would save energy, making the conclusion a bit stronger. If ethanol is less efficient than gas, then we would have to use more ethanol to get the same amount of power. That might mean it takes more energy for the car to go the same distance, making the conclusion weaker. I have "two paths" here.*	C̶

MANHATTAN
PREP

(D) Whether it is possible to produce more ethanol than is currently produced	*The conclusion says we should "increase" the usage of ethanol. But is more ethanol available to use? If we can produce more ethanol, then that makes the argument a bit stronger. If we cannot produce any more ethanol, then how can we increase the usage? That would make the argument weaker.*	D̶
(E) Whether the process of growing corn for fuel would result in as much pollution as does the production of conventional gasoline	*The conclusion claims that using ethanol will reduce pollution, but the argument tells me only that ethanol burns more cleanly than gas. If the process of making ethanol results in less pollution, this would be another point in favor of the conclusion. If the process of making ethanol results in <u>more</u> pollution than does the production of gasoline, however, then this would weaken the conclusion.*	E̶

A̶   Ⓑ   C̶   D̶   E̶

Chapter 7 *of* Critical Reasoning

Evidence Family

In This Chapter...

What Are Inferences?

Inference Questions

Explain a Discrepancy

EXCEPT Questions

Chapter 7
Evidence Family

The Evidence Family of questions is the third main family. Here's a short recap of what you learned about this family in Chapter 2:

- There are no conclusions! Evidence Family questions are made up entirely of premises.
- There are no assumptions either!
- There are two main question types: Inference and Explain a Discrepancy.

Inference questions require you to find a piece of information that *must be true* according to the premises given in the argument.

Explain a Discrepancy questions require you to identify some kind of paradox or puzzling result in an argument and find an answer that explains, or resolves, the puzzling part of the argument. Before delving further into each type, let's talk about what inferences are on the GMAT.

What Are Inferences?

In GMAT World, an inference is something that absolutely *must* be true according to the evidence given in the argument. You don't usually think of inferences this way; rather, in the real world, inferences are *likely* to be true based on the available evidence, but they don't absolutely have to be true. In the real world, an inference is a good guess or conjecture. In GMAT World, an inference is a bulletproof logical consequence.

For example, if a friend tells you that chocolate is her favorite flavor of ice cream, what kind of real-world inferences might you make? You might "infer" that she likes chocolate in general and that she likes ice cream in general. Maybe she likes all desserts in general—perhaps she has a sweet tooth. All of these things are perfectly reasonable to "infer" in the real world, but not a single one *has* to be true. It's possible that she likes chocolate only when it's in the form of ice cream, or that she likes ice cream only when it's chocolate. The kinds of answers discussed in this paragraph would be tempting *incorrect* answers on the GMAT.

What would be good GMAT inferences? Well, what *must* be true? She can't like vanilla ice cream better than she likes chocolate ice cream—if chocolate is her *favorite* flavor of ice cream, then by definition she doesn't like any other flavor better. She has to have tried at least one other flavor of ice cream at some point in her life—she has to have had the ability to compare with at least one other flavor in order to decide that chocolate is her *favorite* flavor. These kinds of inferences would be correct answers on the GMAT.

All inference lessons refer to the GMAT's definition: something that *must* be true based on the available evidence.

Inference Questions

Inference questions require you to find an answer that must be true according to the information in the argument.

Most Inference question stems contain some form of the words "conclude" or "infer," although some variations don't include those specific words. Here are examples of phrasing in Inference questions:

- Which answer can be "logically concluded"?
- The "statements above most strongly support which of the following conclusions"?
- Which answer can be "properly inferred"?
- The statements above "best support" which of the following "assertions"?
- Which answer "must be true" based upon the above statements?

Note: Inference question stems can contain the language "most strongly support," which you also saw on Strengthen questions.

The below diagram shows how to tell whether the word "support" indicates Strengthen or Inference. On Inference questions, the argument (above) is used to support the correct answer (below). On Strengthen questions, the correct answer (below) is used to support the conclusion of the argument (above):

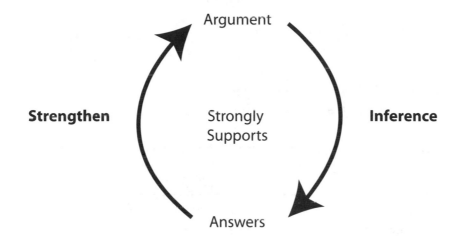

Inference questions will ask you to **use the argument to support an answer choice**. Also, Inference arguments will *not* contain a conclusion in the argument or question stem; they will consist only of premises.

By contrast, **Strengthen** questions will ask you to **use an answer to support the argument**. The correct answer would serve as an additional premise to support the argument's conclusion. Also, Strengthen questions will contain a conclusion in the argument or question stem.

Try this short example:

> Both enrollment and total tuition revenue at Brownsville University have increased during each of the last four years. During the same period, enrollment at Canterbury University has steadily decreased, while total tuition revenue has remained constant.
>
> Which of the following hypotheses is best supported by the statement given?
>
> (A) Brownsville University now collects more total revenue from tuition than does Canterbury University.
> (B) The per-student tuition at Canterbury University has risen over the last four years.
> (C) Brownsville University will continue to increase its revenues as long as it continues to increase enrollment.

7

The question stem uses the word "hypotheses" instead of the more common "conclusions," but it signals the same thing: an Inference question. Your notes might look like this:

4 yrs:
BU: enrol, tuit ↑
CU: enrol ↓, tuit =

(premise)

There are two schools but different trends are happening. BU's enrollment and tuition revenues are both going up. CU's enrollment is going down, but tuition revenues are the same.

State your goal: *This is an Inference question, so I have to find an answer that must be true according to the premises.*

(A) Brownsville University now collects more total revenue from tuition than does Canterbury University.	*Things have certainly been looking up for BU lately, but the argument says nothing about the actual dollar values that the schools are collecting. It's entirely possible that CU still collects more money than BU.*	A̶
(B) The per-student tuition at Canterbury University has risen over the last four years.	*Let's see. "Per-student tuition" = revenues / # of students. CU has the same revenues today, so the numerator stays the same, but fewer students, so the denominator gets smaller. Dividing by a smaller number = a larger number. This must be true! I'll check (C), just in case.*	B̲
(C) Brownsville University will continue to increase its revenues as long as it continues to increase enrollment.	*This might be reasonable to believe in the real world, but it doesn't have to be true. A trend never absolutely has to continue in the future.*	C̶

A̶   Ⓑ   C̶

The argument provides several fact-based premises. (It is also possible to have premises that are somewhat more claim-based.) The correct answer must be true based on those premises, though in this case, you only needed to use the information about Canterbury in order to draw the correct conclusion. Answer (B) didn't use the Brownsville data at all. That's perfectly acceptable; you may need to use only some of the information in the argument, not all of it.

Answer (A) tried to trap you into concluding something based on information you don't have (actual dollar values). Answer (C) is a classic "Real-World Distraction" trap—it might be reasonable to believe that the trend will continue, but nothing says that a trend must continue in the future.

MANHATTAN
PREP

Quick quiz! What can you infer in the below situation?

Imagine two ice cream companies, X and Y. Chocolate ice cream represents 60% of Company X's sales and 50% of Company Y's sales. Clearly, Company X sells more chocolate ice cream than Company Y.

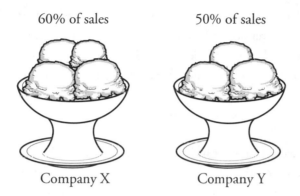

The conclusion above is not necessarily true. You know nothing about the actual sale's numbers, nor about how those percentages relate to each other. What if company Y has $1 million in annual revenues and company X has only $10,000 in annual revenues? In that case, company Y sells a lot more chocolate ice cream than company X. You can't conclude anything about actual dollar amounts from this limited information about percentages.

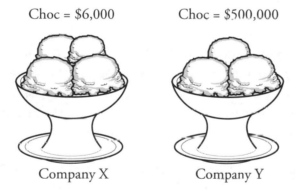

Try this problem:

A particular company sells only vanilla and chocolate ice cream. Last year, 55% of the company's profits were derived from chocolate ice cream sales and 40% of the revenues were derived from vanilla ice cream sales. What can you infer?

(A) Chocolate ice cream is more popular than vanilla ice cream.

(B) The company's vanilla ice cream produces more profit per dollar of sales than does the company's chocolate ice cream.

Yes, they might actually test your math skills on critical reasoning! Because you know that the company sells only these two products, you can figure out two additional percentages. If 55% of profits came from chocolate, then 45% of profits came from vanilla. If 40% of revenues came from vanilla, then 60% of revenues came from chocolate. These things must be true, but these inferences are probably too easy for any GMAT question. What else can you infer?

The company earned 60% of its revenues, but only 55% of its profits, from chocolate. By contrast, the company earned 40% of its revenues and a *higher* percentage of its profits, 45%, from vanilla. That's interesting. The company made more profit on vanilla and less profit on chocolate than you might have expected based on the percentage of revenues that each product generates. *Profitability* is a measure of profit per dollar of revenues. The vanilla ice cream product is more *profitable* than the chocolate ice cream product. That must be true, so answer (B) is correct.

What doesn't have to be true? It doesn't have to be true that vanilla will continue to be more profitable in the future. The trend might not continue. It also doesn't have to be true that more chocolate ice cream is sold by the industry in general—maybe this company makes a fantastic chocolate ice cream, but some other company makes a much better vanilla. Notice that answer (A) focuses on how popular chocolate ice cream is in general, not just this company's chocolate ice cream. You don't have any information about how popular chocolate ice cream is in general.

> When you are given numbers, proportions, or any other mathematical info:
> Confirm whether you have real numbers or percentages.
> Figure out any other values or relationships that must be mathematically true.

Try a full example. Set your timer for two minutes:

> Reducing government spending has been demonstrated to raise the value of a country's currency over time. However, many economists no longer recommend this policy. A currency of lesser value causes a country's exports to be more competitive in the international market, encouraging domestic industries and making the economy more attractive to foreign investment.
>
> The statements above most strongly support which of the following inferences?
>
> (A) Limited government spending can also lead to a reduction in the national deficit.
> (B) Reducing government spending can make a country's exports less competitive.
> (C) Many economists now recommend higher levels of government spending.
> (D) An increase in the value of a currency will result in reduced government spending.
> (E) Competitive exports indicate a weak currency.

Step 1: Identify the question.

The statements above most strongly support which of the following inferences?	*They're asking to support something below (in the answers), and they use the word "inference." This is an Inference question.*	In A B C D E

Step 2: Deconstruct the argument.

Reducing government spending has been demonstrated to raise the value of a country's currency over time.	*This is a fact (that is, I should take it as one in the world of this argument). One thing demonstrably leads to another.*	↓ gov spend → ↑ val curr
However, many economists no longer recommend this policy.	*Hmm. According to the first sentence, raising the value of currency sounds like a good thing, so why wouldn't the economists want to do that?*	BUT econs no longer rec
A currency of lesser value causes a country's exports to be more competitive in the international market, encouraging domestic industries and making the economy more attractive to foreign investment.	*Oh, okay, so there are some good reasons to have a lower currency value. I guess the economists think these benefits outweigh the lower value.*	↓ val curr → exports more > compet → various benefits

Step 3: State the goal.

Reducing government spending will increase currency value. It seems like it would be good to have a high currency value, but some economists disagree, because there are other benefits involved in having a lower currency value.

I need to find an answer that must be true given the information in the argument. I don't need to use all of the info in the argument, though I may.

7

Step 4: Work from wrong to right.

(A) Limited government spending can also lead to a reduction in the national deficit.	*Deficit? This might be reasonable to believe in the real world, but there was nothing about the deficit in the argument—there's no evidence to support this statement.*	A̶
(B) Reducing government spending can make a country's exports less competitive.	*Let's see. The author said that reducing spending leads to a higher currency value. And then the economists said that a lower currency value makes exports more competitive. If that's true, then a higher currency value could make exports less competitive…so it is actually the case that reducing spending might lead to less competitive exports! Keep this one in.*	B̲
(C) Many economists now recommend higher levels of government spending.	*The argument says "many economists" and the answer says "many economists," so that part is okay. If you tell someone not to lower their spending, is that the same thing as telling them to increase their spending? No. You could also recommend spending the same amount. Tricky! This one isn't a "must be true" statement.*	C̶
(D) An increase in the value of a currency will result in reduced government spending.	*This one feels similar to (B)—language pretty similar to the argument, and I have to figure out what leads to what. The author said that X (reducing spending) will lead to Y (a higher currency value). This answer reverses the direction: Y will lead to X. That's not what the author said!*	D̶
(E) Competitive exports indicate a weak currency.	*The economists said that a lower currency value leads to more competitive exports. Hmm. These things do seem to go together, according to the argument. I'll leave this one in and compare it to answer (B).*	Ḛ

7

| Compare (B) and (E). | *Now I need to compare (B) and (E). I'll check the wording of the answers to make sure I'm reading them correctly. Oh, I see. Answer (B) says that reducing spending "can make" exports less competitive, which is true, while (E) says that competitive exports indicate a weak currency. The argument says that a weaker currency leads to more competitive exports, but it doesn't say that the ONLY way to competitive exports is to have a weak currency. Maybe you can have competitive exports by investing in great research and development nationally or in some other fashion, so (E) isn't necessarily true and I can eliminate it.* | B̲ E̲ |

A̶   (B)   C̶   D̶   E̶̲

Common Trap Answers

Real-World Distraction

The most tempting wrong answers on Inference questions tend to revolve around making Real-World Distractions—things that you would reasonably assume to be true in the real world, but, that don't absolutely have to be true. Some of these wrong answers may quite obviously go way too far, but the trickiest ones will seem very reasonable…until you ask yourself whether that answer must be true.

Choices (C) and (E) from the last problem both seem reasonable in the real world, but neither one has to be true. The argument said merely that economists no longer recommend a policy to *reduce* spending. That doesn't necessarily mean that the economists recommend *higher* spending, as choice (C) says. There's also a third option: maintaining the same level of spending. Choice (E) didn't qualify the claim with a "could" or "can." It isn't the case that competitive exports must always indicate a weak currency; they might have been caused by something else.

Reverse Logic

Other wrong answers will use language very similar to the language in the argument but will reverse the proper direction of the information. If you're told that eating honey causes people to hiccup, then a wrong answer might say that hiccupping causes people to eat honey! In the last problem, choice (D) used reverse logic, as did answer choice (E).

Switch Terms

If you're told that the flu often results in weight loss, then a wrong answer might say that illness causes people not to be hungry. All illnesses? The flu is just one example; it isn't reasonable to conclude something about illnesses in general. (In addition, perhaps people are hungry when they have the flu, but they feel so nauseous that they can't eat!)

Explain a Discrepancy

As with Inference questions, Discrepancy questions consist only of premises, mostly on the fact-based side (though it is possible to have more claim-like premises). There are no conclusions. Most of the time, two sets of premises will be presented, and those premises will seem to be contradictory in some way. They won't "make sense" together. Sometimes, the argument will include indicator words such as "surprisingly" or "yet."

Most Discrepancy question stems will include some form of the words "explain" or "resolve" and the vast majority will also contain the words "if true." Here are two typical examples:

> Which of the following, if true, most helps to resolve the paradox described above?

> Which of the following, if true, best explains the fact that many economists no longer recommend reducing spending in order to increase currency values?

Your task on Discrepancy questions is to find an answer that *resolves* or *fixes* the discrepancy—that is, all of the information now makes sense together. If you leave the argument as is, people should say, "Wait. That doesn't make sense." If you add the correct answer into the argument, people should say, "Oh, I see. That makes sense now."

Take a look at this short example:

> According to researchers, low dosages of aspirin taken daily can significantly reduce the risk of heart attack or stroke. Yet doctors have stopped recommending daily aspirin for most patients.
>
> Which of the following, if true, most helps to explain why doctors no longer recommend daily low dosages of aspirin?
>
> (A) Only a small percentage of patients have already experienced a heart attack or stroke.
>
> (B) Patients who are at low risk for heart attack or stroke are less likely to comply with a doctor's recommendation to take aspirin daily.
>
> (C) Aspirin acts as a blood thinner, which can lead to internal bleeding, particularly in the stomach or brain.

The question stem asks you to "explain" something that doesn't make sense: aspirin is apparently beneficial but "doctors have *stopped* recommending" its use for most people (implying that they used to recommend it more). Why would they do that? You might sketch or think of the info visually in this way:

daily aspirin ↓   Drs stop recomm
heart attack, stroke   *BUT*   for most

WHY?

You're trying to highlight the apparent discrepancy between the two facts: on the one hand, daily aspirin is beneficial, and, on the other, doctors have stopped recommending it.

Go back to step 3, and state the goal:

So far, they've told me something really good about taking aspirin daily: it significantly reduces the risk of some pretty bad things. The fact that the doctors have <u>*stopped*</u> *recommending it means that they used to recommend it, so why would they stop doing so? Maybe there's something else that's bad about taking aspirin daily.*

(A) Only a small percentage of patients have already experienced a heart attack or stroke.	*So maybe this means the doctors think it won't help that many people? Wait. The purpose of taking the aspirin is to try to prevent a heart attack or stroke. If most people haven't had a heart attack or stroke, you'd want them to do something that would help lower the risk.*	A
(B) Patients who are at low risk for heart attack or stroke are less likely to comply with a doctor's recommendation to take aspirin daily.	*I can believe this is true in the real world, but is a doctor really going to say, "Oh, I know a lot of people won't take the life-saving medication properly, so I just won't bother to prescribe it." I hope not! Plus, why would they recommend aspirin to people who are at low risk?*	B
(C) Aspirin acts as a blood thinner, which can lead to internal bleeding, particularly in the stomach or brain.	*Oh, this is a bad thing about aspirin—it can cause you to bleed! Yeah, if it could make your brain start bleeding, I can imagine that doctors would want to avoid prescribing it unless there was a really good reason to do so.*	<u>C</u>

A   B   Ⓒ

Answer (C) indicates a bad consequence that can result from taking aspirin. If you add it to the argument, now it's understandable why doctors might be reluctant to have people take aspirin regularly.

Answer (A) talks about the Wrong Group. The argument talks about preventing heart attacks or strokes in the general population, not only among those who have already experienced these maladies.

Answer (B) might be true, but this doesn't explain why doctors would stop recommending aspirin in general. In addition, this choice limits itself to those who are at low risk for heart attack or stroke—why would doctors need to recommend daily aspirin for a group that doesn't have the risk factors?

7

Try another example:

> In a recent poll, 71% of respondents reported that they cast votes in the most recent national election. Voting records show, however, that only 60% of eligible voters actually voted in that election.
>
> Which of the following pieces of evidence, if true, would provide the best explanation for the discrepancy?
>
> (A) The margin of error for the survey was plus or minus 5 percentage points.
> (B) Fifteen percent of the survey's respondents were living overseas at the time of the election.
> (C) Prior research has shown that people who actually do vote are also more likely to respond to polls than those who do not vote.
> (D) Some people who intend to vote are prevented from doing so by last-minute conflicts or other complications.
> (E) People are less likely to respond to a voting poll on the same day that they voted.

Step 1: Identify the question.

Which of the following pieces of evidence, if true, would provide the best explanation for the discrepancy?	*The question stem uses the word "explanation" and explicitly mentions a "discrepancy," so this is an Explain the Discrepancy question.*	ED A B C D E

Step 2: Deconstruct the argument.

In a recent poll, 71% of respondents reported that they cast votes in the most recent national election.	*Pure fact. There was a poll, and 71% of the people who responded said they voted in the last election.*	Poll: 71% voted
Voting records show, however, that only 60% of eligible voters actually voted in that election.	*Okay, that's strange. Records show that only 60% of people who were allowed to vote actually voted.*	BUT records: only 60% of elig voters voted

Step 3: State the goal.

How can it be the case that, when asked, 71% of the people said they voted, but records show only 60% of those who were allowed to vote actually voted? I don't think it would be because some people voted who weren't allowed to—that would technically resolve the discrepancy, but I doubt the GMAT is going to say that! So what could it have been? Maybe some people are remembering incorrectly or mixed up the election in question. Oh, I know! Polls always have a margin of error, so maybe the margin of error accounts for the discrepancy.

Okay, I need to find something that will make the whole thing make sense—it'll explain why 71% said they voted but records showed that only 60% actually voted.

Step 4: Work from wrong to right.

(A) The margin of error for the survey was plus or minus 5 percentage points.	*Margin of error, bingo! Excellent. So the real percentage could've been anywhere from … 71% + 5% to 71% – 5%, which is still 66%. This doesn't go far enough. Still, it's about margin of error. I'm going to keep this one and come back to it later.*	A̰
(B) Fifteen percent of the survey's respondents were living overseas at the time of the election.	*This percentage is larger than the 11% discrepancy mentioned in the argument. But what group are they talking about? Are these the people who did vote, or didn't vote, or some mix of the two? And what does "living overseas" imply? This country might allow people to vote by absentee ballot. This doesn't resolve anything.*	B̶
(C) Prior research has shown that people who actually do vote are also more likely to respond to polls than those who do not vote.	*People who vote are also more likely to respond to a survey. What does that mean? Of the people who responded, more were likely to have been voters than is represented in the overall population. Oh, I see—the survey group was skewed towards those who voted. That's why 71% of that subgroup could have voted while only 60% of the overall population of eligible voters voted. That's better than A—I'll get rid of A.*	A̰ C̰
(D) Some people who intend to vote are prevented from doing so by last-minute conflicts or other complications.	*I'm sure this is true in the real world. How does it affect this argument? The survey took place after the election; it asked people whether they had voted in the past. It doesn't address what people intended to do before the election.*	D̶

7

(E) People are less likely to respond to a voting poll on the same day that they voted.	*I have no idea when the poll was taken, so I can't do much with this. Even if the poll was done the same day as the election, this just highlights the discrepancy—it's even more puzzling now. I would expect the percentage of people who said they voted to be lower than the real percentage because those who didn't vote that day would be more likely to agree to participate in the poll.*	E

The correct answer is (**C**).

A B Ⓒ D E

Common Trap Answers

Half Way

One common wrong answer trap will seem to be on topic because it will address one of the premises, but it won't actually resolve the discrepancy between the two premises. This trap answer only goes Half Way because it doesn't address the discrepancy between the premises. Some of these will more obviously fall short, such as answer (D), while others will be trickier because they just don't go quite far enough, such as answer (A). If answer (A) had said that the margin of error was plus or minus 15 percentage points, it could have been the correct answer.

Reverse Logic

You may also see Reverse Logic traps, where the answer choice actually highlights or even heightens the discrepancy—that is, the choice makes the surprise even more surprising. Answer (E) could fall into this category: if the poll was taken the same day as the election, then the fact that the numbers don't match would be even more puzzling. People probably wouldn't have forgotten how they just voted, so did some of them lie?

7

EXCEPT Questions

As with Assumption Family questions, Evidence Family questions can also be presented in the negative "EXCEPT" format. These are more likely to occur on Discrepancy questions than on Inference questions.

A regular Discrepancy question might read:

> Which of the following, if true, would best help to explain the surprising finding?

An EXCEPT Discrepancy question might read:

> Each of the following, if true, could help to explain the surprising finding EXCEPT:

What is the difference in wording between those two questions?

The first one indicates that one answer choice, and only one, explains the discrepancy. That is the answer choice that you want to pick.

The second one indicates that four answer choices explain the discrepancy. These four are all wrong answers. The fifth answer will NOT explain or resolve the discrepancy. This is the "odd one out" and the correct answer.

Similarly, on an Inference EXCEPT question, four answer choices will represent things that must be true according to the argument; eliminate these four. One answer will represent something that does not have to be true. This is the "odd one out"; pick it!

Cheat Sheets

Inference Cheat Sheet

Identify
the Question

Common:	*conclude*
	infer
Less common:	*assertion*
	hypothesis
	must be true
Infer:	Use argument to support answer.
Strengthen:	Use answer to support conclusion in argument.

Deconstruct
the Argument

Find: Premises
(No conclusion! No assumptions!)

If not sure whether Infer or Strengthen, check the argument for a conclusion. No conclusion = infer.

State the **Goal**

Must be true based on the information given in the argument. Does not need to use all of argument info.

**Work from
Wrong to Right**

Right:	Must be true given the info in the argument.
Wrong:	Real-World Distraction (logical in real world, but not necessarily true based on argument)
	Reverse Direction (says X leads to Y, when really Y leads to X)
	Switch Terms (leads to different meaning: not the right group, object, or idea)

Photocopy this page and keep it with the review sheets you're creating as you study. Better yet, use this page as a guide to create your own review sheet—you'll remember the material better if you write it down yourself.

Explain a Discrepancy

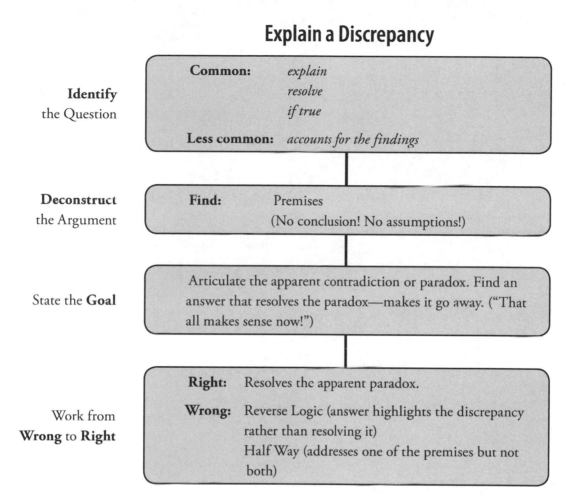

Identify
the Question

Common: *explain*
                resolve
                if true

Less common: *accounts for the findings*

Deconstruct
the Argument

Find: Premises
            (No conclusion! No assumptions!)

State the **Goal**

Articulate the apparent contradiction or paradox. Find an answer that resolves the paradox—makes it go away. ("That all makes sense now!")

Work from
Wrong to **Right**

Right: Resolves the apparent paradox.

Wrong: Reverse Logic (answer highlights the discrepancy rather than resolving it)
            Half Way (addresses one of the premises but not both)

Photocopy this page and keep it with the review sheets you're creating as you study. Better yet, use this page as a guide to create your own review sheet—you'll remember the material better if you write it down yourself.

7

Problem Set

1. *Nitrogen Triiodide*

    Nitrogen triiodide is a highly explosive chemical that is easy to make from only two ingredients: ammonia and concentrated iodine. However, nitrogen triiodide has never been known to be used in a terrorist or criminal attack.

    Which of the following, if true, is the most likely explanation for the discrepancy described above?

    (A) Ammonia can be bought in a grocery store, but concentrated iodine must be obtained from somewhat more restricted sources, such as chemical supply houses.
    (B) Nitrogen triiodide is only one of several powerful explosives that can be made from ammonia.
    (C) Many terrorists and criminals have used other chemical explosives such as TNT or PETN.
    (D) Airport security devices are typically calibrated to detect nitrogen compounds, such as ammonia and ammonium compounds.
    (E) Nitrogen triiodide is extremely shock sensitive and can detonate as a result of even slight movement.

2. *Mycenaean Vase*

    Museum A will display only undamaged objects of proven authenticity. Doubts have been raised about the origins of a supposedly Mycenaean vase currently on display in the museum's antiquities wing. The only way to establish this vase's authenticity would be to pulverize it, then subject the dust to spectroscopic analysis.

    The claims above, if true, most strongly support which of the following conclusions?

    (A) Authentic Mycenaean vases are valuable and rare.
    (B) Museum A has been beset with questions about the provenance of many of the items in its antiquities wing.
    (C) The vase in question will no longer be displayed in Museum A.
    (D) Spectroscopic analysis has revolutionized the forensic investigation of art forgery.
    (E) Knowingly or not, many of the world's museums display some forgeries.

7

3. *Gas Mileage*

The average fuel efficiency of vehicles sold nationwide during the period 2000–2004 was 25 miles per gallon; the corresponding figure during the period 1995–1999 was 20 miles per gallon. The national average price of gasoline during the period 2000–2004 was $2 per gallon; the corresponding figure during the period 1995–1999 was $1.60 per gallon.

The statements above, if true, best support which of the following conclusions?

(A) The average fuel efficiency of vehicles sold nationwide should reach 30 miles per gallon for the period 2005–2009.

(B) The national average price of gasoline during 1997 was lower than the corresponding price during 2003.

(C) Rising gasoline prices led consumers to purchase more fuel-efficient cars.

(D) Between the two described time periods, the national average fuel efficiency and the national average gasoline price both increased at roughly the same rate.

(E) Consumers spent more money on gasoline during the period 2000–2004 than during the period 1995–1999.

4. *CarStore*

CarStore's sales personnel have an average of 15 years' experience selling auto-mobiles, and they regularly sell more cars than other local dealers. Despite this, CarStore has recently implemented a mandatory training program for all sales personnel.

Which of the following, if true, best explains the facts given above?

(A) The sales personnel in CarStore have historically specialized in aggressively selling automobiles and add-on features.

(B) Salespeople at other local dealers average 10 years' experience.

(C) It is common for new or less experienced employees to participate in training programs.

(D) Pricing information, which used to be confidential, has recently been released on the internet, and many customers try to negotiate lower prices using this data.

(E) Several retailers that compete directly with CarStore use "customer-centered" sales approaches.

5. *Stem Cell Research*

Government restrictions have severely limited the amount of stem cell research U.S. companies can conduct. Because of these restrictions, many U.S. scientists who specialize in the field of stem cell research have signed long-term contracts to work for foreign companies. Recently, Congress has proposed lifting all restrictions on stem cell research.

Which of the following statements can most properly be inferred from the information above?

(A)   Some foreign companies that conduct stem cell research work under fewer restrictions than some U.S. companies do.

(B)   Because U.S. scientists are under long-term contracts to foreign companies, there will be a significant influx of foreign professionals into the U.S.

(C)   In all parts of the world, stem cell research is dependent on the financial backing of local government.

(D)   In the near future, U.S. companies will no longer be at the forefront of stem cell research.

(E)   If restrictions on stem cell research are lifted, many of the U.S. scientists will break their contracts to return to U.S. companies.

6. *Hunting Season*

In an effort to reduce the number of deer, and therefore decrease the number of automobile accidents caused by deer, the government lengthened the deer hunting season earlier this year. Surprisingly, the number of accidents caused by deer has increased substantially since the introduction of the longer hunting season.

All of the following, if true, help to explain the increase in traffic accidents caused by deer EXCEPT:

(A)   The presence of humans in the woods causes the deer to move to new areas, which causes the deer to cross roads more frequently than normal.

(B)   In the area where the deer live, traffic has increased substantially precisely because of the lengthened hunting season.

(C)   Most automobile accidents involving deer result from cars swerving to avoid deer, and leave the deer in question unharmed.

(D)   Deer tend to bolt when hearing gunshots or other loud sounds and are more likely to run across a road without warning.

(E)   A new highway was recently built directly through the state's largest forest, which is the primary habitat of the state's deer population.

7

7. *World Bank*

In 2010, China comprised about 10 percent of the world's gross domestic product (GDP), and its voting share in the World Bank was increased from less than 3% to 4.4%. During the same time frame, France comprised about 4% of the world's GDP and saw its voting share in the World bank drop from 4.3% to 3.8%.

Which of the following can be logically concluded from the passage above?

(A) World Bank voting shares are allocated based upon each country's share of the world's GDP.

(B) The new ratio of voting share to percentage of world GDP is lower for China than it is for France.

(C) Gross domestic product is the most important factor in determining voting share at the World Bank.

(D) China should be upset that its voting share does not match its proportion of the world's GDP.

(E) France lost some of its voting share to China because China comprised a larger portion of the world's GDP.

8. *Barcodes*

Two-dimensional barcodes are omni-directional; that is, unlike one-dimensional barcodes, they can be scanned from any direction. Additionally, two-dimensional barcodes are smaller and can store more data than their one-dimensional counterparts. Despite such advantages, two-dimensional barcodes account for a much smaller portion of total barcode usage than one-dimensional barcodes.

Which of the following, if true, most helps to resolve the apparent paradox?

(A) Many smaller stores do not use barcodes at all because of the expense.

(B) For some products, the amount of data necessary to be coded is small enough to fit fully on a one-dimensional barcode.

(C) Two-dimensional barcodes are, on average, less expensive than one-dimensional barcodes.

(D) Two-dimensional barcodes can also be scanned by consumer devices, such as cell phones.

(E) One-dimensional barcodes last longer and are less prone to error than two-dimensional barcodes.

Solutions

1. Nitrogen Triiodide: The correct answer is (E).

Step 1: Identify the question.

Which of the following, if true, is the most likely explanation for the discrepancy described above?	The word "discrepancy" indicates that this is an Explain the Discrepancy question.	ED A B C D E

Step 2: Deconstruct the argument.

Nitrogen triiodide is a highly explosive chemical that is easy to make from only two ingredients: ammonia and concentrated iodine.	This is a fact. I think the main point is that this high explosive is easy to make, not that I need those two specific ingredients, so I'm not going to write them down.	NT expl, easy to make
However, nitrogen triiodide has never been known to be used in a terrorist or criminal attack.	That's weird. If it's so easy to make, why haven't criminals and terrorists used it? Maybe it's hard to get one of the ingredients or they're really expensive?	BUT never used by terr or crims

Step 3: State the goal.

This is a Discrepancy question, so the argument will provide two seemingly contradictory pieces of information. I need to find something that will make everything make sense.

In this case, there's an explosive that's easy to make, and yet criminals have never used it. I need to find something that explains why.

7

Step 4: Work from wrong to right.

(A) Ammonia can be bought in a grocery store, but concentrated iodine must be obtained from somewhat more restricted sources, such as chemical supply houses.	*This is kind of like what I said before—it's harder to get one of the chemicals. This might explain it…except it doesn't say that you can't get iodine. It just says you have to go to a special place, but you can still get it under "somewhat more restricted" conditions. So I'm not sure that really explains why no criminals have ever used it. I'll leave this in until I find something better.*	A̰
(B) Nitrogen triiodide is only one of several powerful explosives that can be made from ammonia.	*So you can make even more explosives from this chemical? That doesn't explain why the criminals have never made it.*	B̶
(C) Many terrorists and criminals have used other chemical explosives such as TNT or PETN.	*Again, this doesn't explain why they haven't used the nitrogen triiodide explosive. Maybe if TNT or PETN are a lot cheaper or easier to make—but this choice doesn't say that.*	C̶
(D) Airport security devices are typically calibrated to detect nitrogen compounds, such as ammonia and ammonium compounds.	*This might explain why no one has tried to bring these explosives into airports, but it doesn't explain why these explosives have never been used in any type of attack anywhere.*	D̶
(E) Nitrogen triiodide is extremely shock sensitive and can detonate as a result of even slight movement.	*Here we go. If the bomb is so unstable that it could go off at any moment, including right after you make it, then it makes sense that criminals don't want to use these explosives. This is better than answer (A).*	A̰ Ḛ

A̰   B   C̶   D̶   Ⓔ

2. Mycenaean Vase: The correct answer is **(C)**.

Step 1: Identify the question.

The claims above, if true, most strongly support which of the following conclusions?	*The language "strongly support" could indicate an Inference or a Strengthen question. The question stem indicates that the answer choice contains the conclusions, though (and the argument didn't have a conclusion), so this is an Inference question.*	In A B C D E

Step 2: Deconstruct the argument.

Museum A will display only undamaged objects of proven authenticity.	*This is a fact—all objects have to be perfect and authenticated for this museum to display them.*	Mus: only perfect, auth objects
Doubts have been raised about the origins of a supposedly Mycenaean vase currently on display in the museum's antiquities wing.	*Another fact: they're not sure whether this vase is authentic.*	Doubts about Myc vase
The only way to establish this vase's authenticity would be to pulverize it, then subject the dust to spectroscopic analysis.	*That's interesting and kind of sad. In order to prove whether the vase is authentic, they've got to destroy it!*	to auth, must destroy!

Step 3: State the goal.

This is an Inference question; I need to find something that must be true according to the info given in the argument. In this case, they're not sure whether this vase is authentic, and the only way to establish its authenticity is to destroy it. But then they can't display it anymore because they'll only display it if it's perfect!

Step 4: Work from wrong to right.

(A) Authentic Mycenaean vases are valuable and rare.	*This might be true, but it doesn't have to be true. The argument says nothing about value or rarity.*	A
(B) Museum A has been beset with questions about the provenance of many of the items in its antiquities wing.	*The argument is only about one particular vase. Any other items are not relevant.*	B
(C) The vase in question will no longer be displayed in Museum A.	*This is exactly what I said before! If they try to authenticate it, they'll destroy the vase, in which case they can't display it. And if they don't try to authenticate it, then they won't know whether it's authentic, in which case Museum A still won't display it. This has to be true (though I'll check the other two answers to be sure).*	C
(D) Spectroscopic analysis has revolutionized the forensic investigation of art forgery.	*This might be true, but it doesn't have to be true that it "revolutionized" the field. It just has to work in general.*	D
(E) Knowingly or not, many of the world's museums display some forgeries.	*I can believe that this is probably true, but it doesn't absolutely have to be true.*	E

A   B   Ⓒ   D   E

3. Gas Mileage: The correct answer is **(D)**.

Step 1: Identify the question.

The statements above, if true, best support which of the following conclusions?	*The language "best support" could indicate an Inference or a Strengthen question. I'm confirming that it's the passage supporting a conclusion in the answer choices, though (and the argument didn't have a conclusion), so this is an Inference question.*	In A B C D E

Step 2: Deconstruct the argument.

The average fuel efficiency of vehicles sold nationwide during the period 2000–2004 was 25 miles per gallon; the corresponding figure during the period 1995–1999 was 20 miles per gallon.	*These are all facts, which I'm expecting because this is an Inference question. They're talking about time periods and figures, so maybe a table is the best way to keep track.*	**95–99**	**00–04**
		Fuel eff 20 mpg	25
The national average price of gasoline during the period 2000–2004 was $2 per gallon; the corresponding figure during the period 1995–1999 was $1.60 per gallon.	*Yep, a table was a good idea! More facts and figures for the same time frame.*	$1.60 per gal	$2

Step 3: State the goal.

This is an Inference question, so I'm looking for something that must be true based on all this data. I was given specific figures for average fuel efficiency and average gas price for two time periods. Both went up over time. I imagine that I'll need to make a mathematical inference.

Step 4: Work from wrong to right.

(A) The average fuel efficiency of vehicles sold nationwide should reach 30 miles per gallon for the period 2005–2009.	*"Should reach?" That doesn't have to be true. Who knows what's going to happen in the future?*	A̶
(B) The national average price of gasoline during 1997 was lower than the corresponding price during 2003.	*The data given is only for the 5-year periods 95–99 and 00–04. I have no idea what the numbers were for 1997 and 2003 specifically.*	B̶
(C) Rising gasoline prices led consumers to purchase more fuel-efficient cars.	*That might be true, but it doesn't have to be true. The argument doesn't say anything about why consumers decide to purchase certain cars.*	C̶
(D) Between the two described time periods, the national average fuel efficiency and the national average gasoline price both increased at roughly the same rate.	*Increased at the same rate? Hmm. I don't know, but I can calculate based on the figures I was already given. The fuel efficiency figure went from 20 to 25. The increase, then, was 5 over a base (or starting point) of 20; 5/20 = 1/4, for a growth rate of 25%. Meanwhile, the price went from 1.6 to 2, which is an increase of 0.4 over a starting point of 1.6; 0.4/1.6 = 1/4, for a growth rate of 25% again. Hey, this is true!*	D̰
(E) Consumers spent more money on gasoline during the period 2000–2004 than during the period 1995–1999.	*Tricky! This one seems pretty good at first glance, but average price per gallon is not the same thing as total amount of money spent. It's true that the average price was higher, but maybe people bought fewer gallons of gasoline (especially because fuel efficiency was better!). This one might be true, but it doesn't have to be.*	E̶

A̶   B̶   C̶   Ⓓ   E̶

4. CarStore: The correct answer is **(D)**.

Step 1: Identify the question.

Which of the following, if true, best explains the facts given above?	*The language "best explains the facts" is a slightly unusual form for a Discrepancy question.*	ED A B C D E

Step 2: Deconstruct the argument.

CarStore's sales personnel have an average of 15 years' experience selling automobiles, and they regularly sell more cars than other local dealers.	*CarStore's people have 15 years' experience on average, and they sell more cars than the competition. These are facts.*	Sales ppl: avg 15y exper, sell more than comp
Despite this, CarStore has recently implemented a mandatory training program for all sales personnel.	*Here's the contrast. Why are they going to make them all go through training? Maybe something has changed in the marketplace?*	BUT store now req training for all

Step 3: State the goal.

This is a Discrepancy question, so I need to find an answer that explains why these two facts are actually NOT contradictory after all. What would explain why CarStore is requiring its employees to go through new training? Maybe something has changed in the marketplace that would require new training.

Step 4: Work from wrong to right.

(A) The sales personnel in CarStore have historically specialized in aggressively selling automobiles and add-on features.	*If CarStore wants to change the way their people sell cars, then new training would make sense…but this choice just talks about what they've done in the past, not what they want to do in the future. This doesn't explain the discrepancy.*	A
(B) Salespeople at other local dealers average 10 years' experience.	*So the CarStore people are more experienced, on average, than other salespeople in the area. If anything, this just accentuates the discrepancy: why do the more experienced people need training?*	B
(C) It is common for new or less experienced employees to participate in training programs.	*This makes sense, but again does not explain why the employees who average 15 years' experience need training. The argument said that all sales personnel have to undergo the training, not just the new ones.*	C̶
(D) Pricing information, which used to be confidential, has recently been released on the internet, and many customers try to negotiate lower prices using this data.	*Ah, so the situation has changed. Customers now know some info that used to be confidential. That might change negotiations, so it makes sense that the salespeople might need new training.*	D

MANHATTAN
PREP

(E) Several retailers that compete directly with CarStore use "customer-centered" sales approaches.	*That's what they already use—the answer doesn't indicate that anything has changed. Nor does it indicate that CarStore doesn't use a customer-centered approach or that consumers prefer a customer-centered approach. This doesn't explain why the CarStore people need training.*	E

A̶   B̶   C̶   Ⓓ   E̶

5. Stem Cell Research: The correct answer is (**A**).

Step 1: Identify the question.

Which of the following statements can most properly be inferred from the information above?	*The word "inferred" indicates that this is an Inference question.*	In A B C D E

Step 2: Deconstruct the argument.

Government restrictions have severely limited the amount of stem cell research U.S. companies can conduct.	*This is a fact. The U.S. government restricts this stem cell research.*	In A B C D E Stem cell res restrict by U.S. gov
Because of these restrictions, many U.S. scientists who specialize in the field of stem cell research have signed long-term contracts to work for foreign companies.	*"Because of" that—so the first sentence leads to the second sentence.*	→ U.S. sci work foreign coms instead
Recently, Congress has proposed lifting all restrictions on stem cell research.	*Still a fact: the government is considering lifting the restrictions. Maybe that'll bring the scientists back to work for U.S. companies?*	U.S. gov: maybe lift restrict?

Step 3: State the goal.

This is an Inference question, so I need to find something that must be true based on the info given so far. The U.S. government restricts a certain kind of research, so many US scientists who do this type of research are working for foreign companies instead. Congress might lift the restrictions.

Step 4: Work from wrong to right.

(A) Some foreign companies that conduct stem cell research work under fewer restrictions than some U.S. companies do.	*If the researchers decided to work for foreign companies specifically <u>because</u> the U.S. companies had restrictions, then that would mean that at least some foreign companies did have fewer restrictions. Yes, this one must be true! I'll check the other answers just in case, though.*	A̰
(B) Because U.S. scientists are under long-term contracts to foreign companies, there will be a significant influx of foreign professionals into the U.S.	*This might be true, but it certainly doesn't have to be true. The argument doesn't say anything about foreign professionals coming into the United States.*	B̶
(C) In all parts of the world, stem cell research is dependent on the financial backing of local government.	*The argument doesn't say anything about how this type of research gets its financial backing. This doesn't have to be true.*	C̶
(D) In the near future, U.S. companies will no longer be at the forefront of stem cell research.	*Irrelevant. The argument doesn't discuss who is or will be at the forefront of this kind of research.*	D̶
(E) If restrictions on stem cell research are lifted, many of the U.S. scientists will break their contracts to return to U.S. companies.	*Maybe this will happen, but it doesn't have to happen. It isn't easy to break a contract.*	E̶

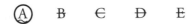

Ⓐ   B̶   C̶   D̶   E̶

6. Hunting Season: The correct answer is (**C**).

Step 1: Identify the question.

All of the following, if true, help to explain the increase in traffic accidents caused by deer EXCEPT:	*The language "help to explain" indicates that this is a Discrepancy question. This is also an EXCEPT question.*	ED Ex A B C D E

Step 2: Deconstruct the argument.

In an effort to reduce the number of deer, and therefore decrease the number of automobile accidents caused by deer, the government lengthened the deer hunting season earlier this year.	*Multiple levels here. First, the government lengthened the hunting season, which is supposed to reduce the number of deer, which is then supposed to reduce the number of car accidents caused by deer.*	Gov: ↑ hunt seas → ↓ deer → ↓ car accids
Surprisingly, the number of accidents caused by deer has increased substantially since the introduction of the longer hunting season.	*That's weird. The exact opposite has happened: there have been more car accidents caused by deer!*	BUT # car acc ↑

Step 3: State the goal.

This is a Discrepancy EXCEPT question. Normally on Discrepancy questions, I'm looking for the answer that makes the contradictory evidence make sense. On this one, though, all four wrong answers will fix the discrepancy. The "odd one out"—the one that doesn't fix the discrepancy—will be the right answer.

So I need to find (and cross off) four things that explain why there have been even more car accidents caused by deer.

Step 4: Work from wrong to right.

(A) The presence of humans in the woods causes the deer to move to new areas, which causes the deer to cross roads more frequently than normal.	*If hunting season is lengthened, then there will be people in the woods for a longer period of time. According to this choice, that means the deer are going to cross the roads more frequently than they otherwise would have. That could increase the likelihood of accidents due to deer, which explains the discrepancy. Cross this one off.*	A̶
(B) In the area where the deer live, traffic has increased substantially precisely because of the lengthened hunting season.	*Oh, this makes sense. The lengthened hunting season actually caused more traffic, so there are more chances for accidents between cars and deer where the deer live. This explains the discrepancy, too.*	B̶
(C) Most automobile accidents involving deer result from cars swerving to avoid deer, and leave the deer in question unharmed.	*This one is tricky! It sounded like it explained the discrepancy when I first read it, but then I realized something: it's just explaining how the accidents tend to happen, but it doesn't address why there are __more__ accidents now than there used to be.*	C̲

(D) Deer tend to bolt when hearing gunshots or other loud sounds and are more likely to run across a road without warning.	*Ah, so if there are gunshots for a longer length of time, then there are more chances for the deer to bolt and cross the road suddenly…increasing the chances of an accident.*	~~D~~
(E) A new highway was recently built directly through the state's largest forest, which is the primary habitat of the state's deer population.	*The situation has changed from the year before: a new highway was built right through the area where the deer live. So it would make sense that there are now more accidents caused by deer.*	~~E~~

~~A~~   ~~B~~   Ⓒ   ~~D~~   ~~E~~

7. World Bank: The correct answer is **(B)**.

Step 1: Identify the question.

Which of the following can be logically concluded from the passage above?	*The language "logically concluded" indicates that this is an Inference question.*	In A B C D E

Step 2: Deconstruct the argument.

In 2010, China comprised about 10% of the world's gross domestic product (GDP), and its voting share in the World Bank was increased from less than 3% to 4.4%.	*A bunch of stats about China in 2010. I just need to keep this straight because, glancing down, I can see the next sentence has more numbers.*	<table><tr><td>2010</td><td>GDP</td><td>Vote Share</td></tr><tr><td>China</td><td>10</td><td><3 → 4.4</td></tr></table>
During the same time frame, France comprised about 4% of the world's GDP and saw its voting share in the World bank drop from 4.3% to 3.8%.	*Same type of stats, but about France this time. Same time frame.*	<table><tr><td>Fra</td><td>4</td><td>4.3 → 3.8</td></tr></table>

Step 3: State the goal.

This is an Inference question, so I need to find something that must be true based upon the info given so far. There are a lot of numbers to keep straight, but generally, China has a larger share of the world GDP than France. China used to have a lower voting share than France, but now it has a higher share.

MANHATTAN
PREP

Step 4: Work from wrong to right.

(A) World Bank voting shares are allocated based upon each country's share of the world's GDP.	*Maybe. It is the case now that China has a larger GDP and a larger voting share. But it didn't used to be that way. And I only have two data points; I don't know the numbers with all of the other countries. This doesn't have to be true.*	A
(B) The new ratio of voting share to percentage of world GDP is lower for China than it is for France.	*Let's see. China's ratio is 4.4 / 10. And the ratio for France is 3.8 / 4. The first number is a lot smaller than the second number: the first one is 0.44 and the second one is almost 1. So, yes, it's true that China's ratio is lower than France's.*	B̰
(C) Gross domestic product is the most important factor in determining voting share at the World Bank.	*"Most important?" The argument didn't say anything about how voting share is determined or which factor is most important.*	C̶
(D) China should be upset that its voting share does not match its proportion of the world's GDP.	*China might be upset but this doesn't have to be true—and it doesn't have to be true that China "should" be upset. That's a judgment call.*	D̶
(E) France lost some of its voting share to China because China comprised a larger portion of the world's GDP.	*Maybe this is true, but they didn't actually say why the voting shares were changed. I could speculate, but this doesn't have to be true.*	E̶

A̶   Ⓑ   C̶   D̶   E̶

8. Barcodes: The correct answer is **(E)**.

Step 1: Identify the question.

Which of the following, if true, most helps to resolve the apparent paradox?	*The word "paradox" indicates that this is a Discrepancy question.*	ED A B C D E

Step 2: Deconstruct the argument.

Two-dimensional barcodes are omni-directional; that is, unlike one-dimensional barcodes, they can be scanned from any direction.	*Okay, so 2D barcodes have a better feature than 1D barcodes.*	2D barcodes scan any dir, unlike 1D
Additionally, two-dimensional barcodes are smaller and can store more data than their one-dimensional counterparts.	*Even more advantages for the 2D barcodes.*	Also 2D smaller, more data

Despite such advantages, two-dimensional barcodes account for a much smaller portion of total barcode usage than one-dimensional barcodes.	*But the 1D barcodes are used a lot more—why? There must be some advantages to the 1Ds or disadvantages for the 2Ds that I don't yet know about.*	BUT 1D is used >>

Step 3: State the goal.

I need to find something that fixes the discrepancy described in the argument: the 2D barcodes have a bunch of advantages, but people mostly still use the 1D barcodes. Why? Maybe the 2D ones are super-expensive or something like that.

Step 4: Work from wrong to right.

(A) Many smaller stores do not use barcodes at all because of the expense.	*Expense—does this explain why 1D barcodes are still being used? No, wait—this says the stores aren't using any type of barcode at all. So that doesn't explain why the ones who do use barcodes seem to prefer the 1D models.*	A̶
(B) For some products, the amount of data necessary to be coded is small enough to fit fully on a one-dimensional barcode.	*Okay, so some products might not need the 2D barcodes. Except, this only mentions "some" products, while the argument says that the 2D barcodes are a "much smaller" portion of total usage. This doesn't fully explain the discrepancy.*	B̶
(C) Two-dimensional barcodes are, on average, less expensive than one-dimensional barcodes.	*Less expensive, this is it! Wait a second. No, this says the 2D barcodes are less expensive—that gives them yet another advantage! If they're less expensive, I'd expect people to use them more. This isn't it.*	C̶
(D) Two-dimensional barcodes can also be scanned by consumer devices, such as cell phones.	*This sounds like yet another advantage for the 2D barcodes. This isn't it either!*	D̶
(E) One-dimensional barcodes last longer and are less prone to error than two-dimensional barcodes.	*Here are two advantages for the 1D barcodes. If it's true that they last longer and are less prone to error, then that would explain why people would want to use them rather than the 2D barcodes.*	E̲

A̶   B̶   C̶   D̶   Ⓔ

Chapter 8 *of* Critical Reasoning

Wrong Answer Analysis

In This Chapter...

No Tie to the Argument

Reverse Logic

The Diversion

Close but No Cigar

Chapter 8
Wrong Answer Analysis

In previous chapters, you learned about all of the question types along with their common traps or wrong answer types. This chapter is a summary of the "wrong answer" information scattered throughout the question-types chapters, and it also contains additional examples to illustrate the characteristics of these common traps.

The multiple different wrong-answer types are grouped into four big categories:

1. No Tie to the Argument

2. Reverse Logic

3. The Diversion

4. Close but No Cigar

No Tie to the Argument (variant: No Tie to the Conclusion)

This wrong answer type is most commonly found in the five Assumption Family question types: Find the Assumption, Strengthen the Argument, Weaken the Argument, Evaluate the Argument, and Find the Flaw.

Assumption Family question types all contain premises and a conclusion, known collectively as the author's argument. For each of the question types, the correct answer has to affect the overall argument in a specific way. If the choice does not actually affect that argument, then it must be wrong.

Consider this example:

> In order to improve retention of the most productive employees, Q Corp plans to allocate the bonus pool in such a way that the longest-serving employees will earn the highest bonuses.

Which of the following, if true, would strengthen the claim that Q Corp's plan will succeed?

(A)   Q Corp also plans to improve healthcare benefits.

(B)   The most productive employees have been with Q Corp an average of 13 years, which is longer than the average employee tenure at the company.

The argument is not just that Q Corp wants to improve employee retention in general. The argument is the *entire plan*: Q Corp will allocate bonuses in a certain way in order to improve employee retention.

The bonus plan will clearly reward the people who have been there the longest. Are they also the most productive employees? Choice (B) bridges this gap by indicating that the most productive employees have indeed worked for the company for a long time.

Note that this choice does not make Q Corp's plan perfect. It's possible that some very productive employees have not been at the company that long, but overall, the plan is more *likely* to be valid. This standard (more likely to be valid) is all that is required for a Strengthen question.

Choice (A) is tempting because it is reasonable to think that improving other benefits will help the over-all goal of improving retention of the most productive employees. This might very well be true—but the question doesn't ask you to come up with ways to reach the overall goal. Rather, it asks you to strengthen the *given argument*: that this plan will work in the way described. Choice (A) doesn't say anything about the given plan. It has No Tie to the Argument.

Some questions are part of a subset of this wrong answer type; they have No Tie to the Conclusion (as opposed to the overall argument or plan). In these cases, a choice might address a premise of the argument but it may have no impact on the conclusion, specifically.

Take a look at this example:

Question	"No Tie to the Conclusion" Wrong Answer
Which of the following, if true, best supports the claim that women who are under 5 feet 10 inches tall cannot have successful careers as basketball players?	Some women who are over 5 feet 10 inches tall are likely to excel at basketball.

In many ways, the wrong answer seems relevant: it's talking about women and basketball; it mentions the "5 feet 10 inch" height threshold. It does not, however, provide any information about women who are under 5 feet 10 inches tall. The conclusion claimed something about this *specific* group of women. If the answer on a Strengthen the Conclusion question does not actually address the given conclusion, then it has No Tie to the Conclusion.

8

Reverse Logic

One of the most tempting traps is the Reverse Logic trap, when you accidentally pick the opposite of what you really want, such as an answer that strengthens on a Weaken question. Reverse Logic traps occur most frequently on Assumption Family and Evidence Family questions.

One of the most common ways in which you fall into this trap is to misidentify the conclusion, particularly when the argument contains two "sides," or points of view. Consider this example:

> Some companies tie bonuses to company performance as well as personal performance, on the theory that individual performance is only valuable as far as it benefits the company as a whole. This is counterproductive, however, because the highest-performing employees are essentially penalized by receiving a bonus commensurate only with the average performance of the overall company, thereby leading to a lack of motivation to continue to outperform their peers.

What are the claims here? Some companies think that "individual performance is only valuable if it benefits the company as a whole" and set up their bonus plans accordingly. Some unknown person, on the other hand, thinks that this viewpoint is "counterproductive" and will "[lead] to a lack of motivation" on the part of the best employees. Which is the main conclusion?

The author's point of view is always the main conclusion. In this case, the "unknown person" is the author. If a claim is attributed to a particular person or group, that claim is likely *not* the author's claim. A claim that is simply asserted, with no commentary as to who is doing the asserting, must be the author's claim.

It would be easy to mix up the claims, though, and that in turn would make it easy to pick a Reverse Logic answer, since the two claims are on opposing sides of the fence.

Consider this problem, using the same argument:

> Some companies tie bonuses to company performance as well as personal performance, on the theory that individual performance is only valuable as far as it benefits the company as a whole in some way. This is counterproductive, however, because the highest-performing employees are essentially penalized by receiving a bonus commensurate only with the average performance of the overall company, thereby leading to a lack of motivation to continue to outperform their peers.
>
> Which of the following, if true, would most seriously undermine the argument above?
>
> (A) The performance of employees who feel they aren't appropriately compensated for their efforts often drops.
>
> (B) High-performing employees typically state that their primary motivation is the satisfaction of a job well done.

In this example, choice (A) strengthens the conclusion instead of weakening it (and it is even easier to fall into this trap if you misidentify the conclusion!). The correct answer, on the other hand, does weaken the author's conclusion by offering a reason why employees might continue to work hard regardless of compensation levels.

The Diversion

Some answers try to mix you up by emphasizing a distracting point or switching terms around to muddle the message. Three wrong answer types fall into this category.

1. Irrelevant Distinction

Consider this argument:

> Students who earn A and B grades are more likely to participate in sports than are students who earn C grades. Therefore, participation in sports helps students achieve higher grades.

You're asked to find an assumption. An incorrect answer might say something like:

> Students who earn A grades participate in sports more frequently than those who earn B grades.

The answer separates, or makes a distinction between, the A and B students. But the argument grouped together the grade-A and grade-B students; it treated them in the same way! The distinction was between those two sets of students and the C students. The answer is an example of an irrelevant distinction; the differences between A and B students don't matter to the argument as given.

These wrong answers tend to show up the most in Assumption Family questions.

2. Real-World Distraction

Tricky wrong answers on Inference questions will try to distract you with reasonable-sounding information that might seem true in the real world. However, the correct Inference answer must be proven using the information in the argument. You cannot prove any wrong answer, as tempting as it may seem.

8

MANHATTAN
PREP

For example:

> Teachers who switch careers are most likely to leave the teaching profession in their third year of teaching. A majority of teachers who remain in the profession for at least seven years stick with teaching for the remainder of their careers.
>
> Which of the following conclusions can most properly be drawn from the information above?
>
> (A) Most teachers who leave the profession do so because the work is very stressful and the pay poor.
>
> (B) A majority of teachers who leave the profession do so within three years of beginning to teach.
>
> (C) A teacher in his or her sixth year of teaching is more likely to remain in the profession than one who is in his or her third year of teaching.

Choices (A) and (B) are both Real-World Distractions. You've probably known at least one teacher who complained about the stress level and pay for the job. You might even have read statistics showing that a high percentage of teachers do leave the profession in the first three years on the job (though the real number is below half). However, neither of those things can be proven from the given argument.

At first, answer choice (C) might seem wrong because it mentions a year that isn't mentioned in the argument. This choice can actually be proven true, though. The third year is the year in which a teacher is *most* likely to leave the profession. Therefore, a teacher in the sixth year (or second year, or twentieth year of his or her career) must be less likely to leave than the one in his or her third year.

3. Switching Terms

Some tempting wrong answers will switch terms on you. The answer choice will use actual wording or terminology from the argument but will switch the terms around or pair things that weren't actually paired in the argument. For instance, consider the following statement; what can you infer?

> Studies have shown that holding a blood drive tends to stimulate the participation of members of an organization and increase the number of donations.
>
> (A) Holding a blood drive helps an organization to increase the number of members.

Match the terms. The argument says that the blood drive will increase the number of *donations*, not the number of *members*. Trap answer (A) switched terms! It might be true that the blood drive also increases the number of members, but the argument doesn't indicate anything of the sort! The argument indicates only that the member *participation* is stimulated.

8

An argument might also use something that seems like a synonym but isn't. For example, an argument might talk about art. One of the answer choices might talk about a museum. Museums do contain art, so that might be okay, but it might not—you need to check whether museums are actually relevant or whether the answer is just trying to get you to think so because museums do have something to do with art. Synonyms are okay if they do actually match the overall argument, but they can also be used as traps.

Close but No Cigar

The final major category consists of those answers that are oh-so-close, but not quite right. These tend to show up most on Structure Family or Explain a Discrepancy questions.

One Word Off

The One Word Off variety is simple, in the sense that only one or two words are off. These are also quite difficult and tempting, though, because only a single word could make the difference!

For example, what's the difference between the two answer choices below?

> The first is a prediction that supports a position that the argument concludes.

> The first is a prediction that supports a position that the argument opposes.

Only one word is different—the very last word—and yet that one word changes everything. The first sample answer is describing a premise: something that supports the author's conclusion. The second, on the other hand, is describing a counterpremise: something that *goes against* the author's conclusion. If you're reading too quickly or skim over a word, that can be the difference between picking the right answer and falling for a tempting trap.

Half Right

Answers to Describe the Role questions might be Half Right. For instance, an answer could accurately describe the first boldface statement but not the second. Explain the Paradox questions can have a similar problem: the correct answer might address one half of the apparent paradox but not the other half. It's impossible to explain a paradox without addressing both halves, so don't pick an answer that addresses only one half!

In short, Half Right is just as wrong as all wrong, so make sure to read each answer choice thoroughly.

8

Wrong Answer Traps

Keep a running list for yourself of the definitions of the wrong answer traps. You'll remember these better if you create a version using your own words.

Question Types:

Assumption Family: Find the Assumption, Strengthen the Argument, Weaken the Argument, Evaluate the Argument, Find the Flaw

Evidence Family: Inference, Explain a Discrepancy

Structure Family: Describe the Role, Describe the Argument

No Tie (most common: Assumption Family)	No Tie to Argument	The answer choice does not affect the overall argument.
	No Tie to Conclusion	The answer choice does not affect the conclusion.
Reverse Logic (most common: Assumption and Evidence Families)	Reverse Logic	Does the opposite of what you want! For example, it strengthens rather than weakens.
The Diversion	Irrelevant Distinction (most common: Assumption Family)	Makes a distinction or comparison between two things that are not necessary to distinguish or compare.
	Real-World Distraction (most common: Inference)	Sounds good in the real world, but the argument doesn't say so.
	Switching Terms	Mixes up actual terms from the argument in a way that changes the meaning. Alternatively, may use synonyms that are too "loose"—check that any synonyms do fit the argument.
Close but No Cigar (most common: Structure Family; Explain a Discrepancy)	One Word Off	Almost right but one or two words mess it up. Read every word!
	Half Right	Does only half of what it should do. For example, it describes one boldface statement correctly but not the other.

8

Problem Set

The problem set consists of problems that you have already seen in earlier chapters of this book. Note: if you have not yet done these problems, then do them normally under the two-minute time constraint for the first time before doing the exercise described below.

For each of the following problems, identify the right answer, and try to articulate *why* each wrong answer is wrong. If you spot a particular category of wrong answer, write that down as well, but remember that the real test won't ask you to classify. Rather, your goal is to train yourself to be able to identify wrong answers accurately and efficiently; the wrong answer categories are just a tool to help you practice this. Also note that some wrong answers may not fit into any of the common categories listed in this chapter.

1. *Gray Wolf Population*
From Chapter 3, Structure Family

> Government representative: Between 1996 and 2005, the gray wolf population in Minnesota grew nearly 50%; the gray wolf population In Montana increased by only 13% during the same period. Clearly, the Minnesota gray wolf population is more likely to survive and thrive long term.

> Environmentalist: But the gray wolf population in Montana is nearly 8 times the population in Minnesota; above a certain critical breeding number, the population is stable and does not require growth in order to survive.

> The environmentalist challenges the government representative's argument by doing which of the following?

> (A) Introducing additional evidence that undermines an assumption made by the representative
>
> (B) Challenging the representative's definition of a critical breeding number
>
> (C) Demonstrating that the critical breeding number of the two wolf populations differs significantly
>
> (D) Implying that the two populations of wolves could be combined in order to preserve the species
>
> (E) Suggesting that the Montana wolf population grew at a faster rate than stated in the representative's argument

8

2. *Malaria*

From Chapter 3, Structure Family

In an attempt to explain the cause of malaria, a deadly infectious disease, early European settlers in Hong Kong attributed the malady to poisonous gases supposedly emanating from low-lying swampland. In the 1880s, however, doctors determined that Anopheles mosquitoes were responsible for transmitting the disease to humans after observing that **the female of the species can carry a parasitic protozoan that is passed on to unsuspecting humans when a mosquito feasts on a person's blood.**

What function does the statement in boldface fulfill with respect to the argument presented above?

(A) It provides support for the explanation of a particular phenomenon.

(B) It presents evidence that contradicts an established fact.

(C) It offers confirmation of a contested assumption.

(D) It identifies the cause of an erroneous conclusion.

(E) It proposes a new conclusion in place of an earlier conjecture.

3. *Oil and Ethanol*

From Chapter 4, Find the Assumption

Country N's oil production is not sufficient to meet its domestic demand. In order to sharply reduce its dependence on foreign sources of oil, Country N recently embarked on a program requiring all of its automobiles to run on ethanol in addition to gasoline. Combined with its oil production, Country N produces enough ethanol from agricultural by-products to meet its current demand for energy.

Which of the following must be assumed in order to conclude that Country N will succeed in its plan to reduce its dependence on foreign oil?

(A) Electric power is not a superior alternative to ethanol in supplementing automobile gasoline consumption.

(B) In Country N, domestic production of ethanol is increasing more quickly than domestic oil production.

(C) Ethanol is suitable for the heating of homes and other applications aside from automobiles.

(D) In Country N, gasoline consumption is not increasing at a substantially higher rate than domestic oil and ethanol production.

(E) Ethanol is as efficient as gasoline in terms of mileage per gallon when used as fuel for automobiles.

8

MANHATTAN
PREP

4. *Charity*

From Chapter 4, Find the Assumption

> Studies show that impoverished families give away a larger percentage of their income in charitable donations than do wealthy families. As a result, fundraising consultants recommend that charities direct their marketing efforts toward individuals and families from lower socioeconomic classes in order to maximize the dollar value of incoming donations.
>
> Which of the following best explains why the consultants' reasoning is flawed?

(A) Marketing efforts are only one way to solicit charitable donations.

(B) Not all impoverished families donate to charity.

(C) Some charitable marketing efforts are so expensive that the resulting donations fail to cover the costs of the marketing campaign.

(D) Percentage of income is not necessarily indicative of absolute dollar value.

(E) People are more likely to donate to the same causes to which their friends donate.

5. *Food Allergies*

From Chapter 6, Evaluate the Argument and Find the Flaw

> Food allergies account for more than 30,000 emergency department visits each year. Often, victims of these episodes are completely unaware of their allergies until they experience a major reaction. Studies show that 90% of food allergy reactions are caused by only eight distinct foods. For this reason, individuals should sample a minuscule portion of each of these foods to determine whether a particular food allergy is present.
>
> Which of the following must be studied in order to evaluate the recommendation made in the argument?

(A) The percentage of allergy victims who were not aware of the allergy before a major episode

(B) The percentage of the population that is at risk for allergic reactions

(C) Whether some of the eight foods are common ingredients used in cooking

(D) Whether an allergy to one type of food makes someone more likely to be allergic to other types of food

(E) Whether ingesting a very small amount of an allergen is sufficient to provoke an allergic reaction in a susceptible individual

6. *Smithtown Theatre*

From Chapter 5, Strengthen and Weaken

> The Smithtown Theatre, which stages old plays, has announced an expansion that will double its capacity along with its operating costs. The theatre is only slightly profitable at present. In addition, all of the current customers live in Smithtown, and the population of the town is not expected to increase in the next several years. Thus, the expansion of the Smithtown Theatre will prove unprofitable.

Which of the following, if true, would most seriously weaken the argument?

(A) A large movie chain plans to open a new multiplex location in Smithtown later this year.

(B) Concession sales in the Smithtown Theatre comprise a substantial proportion of the theatre's revenues.

(C) Many recent arrivals to Smithtown are students who are less likely to attend the Smithtown Theatre than are older residents.

(D) The expansion would allow the Smithtown Theatre to stage larger, more popular shows that will attract customers from neighboring towns.

(E) The Board of the Smithtown Theatre often solicits input from residents of the town when choosing which shows to stage.

7. *Digital Coupons*

From Chapter 5, Strengthen and Weaken

> The redemption rate for e-mailed coupons is far lower than that for traditionally distributed paper coupons. One factor is the "digital divide"—those who might benefit the most from using coupons, such as homemakers, the elderly, and those in low-income households, are less likely to have the knowledge or equipment necessary to go online and receive coupons.

Which of the following, if true, does the most to support the claim that the digital divide is responsible for lower electronic coupon redemption rates?

(A) Computers are available for free in libraries, schools, and community centers.

(B) The redemption rate of ordinary coupons is particularly high among elderly and low-income people who do not know how to use computers.

(C) Many homes, including those of elderly and low-income people, do not have high-speed internet connections.

(D) More homemakers than elderly people would use computers if they had access to them.

(E) The redemption rate for coupons found on the internet has risen in the last five years.

MANHATTAN
PREP

8.   *World Bank*

From Chapter 7, Evidence Family

> In 2010, China comprised about 10% of the world's gross domestic product (GDP), and its voting share in the World Bank was increased from less than 3% to 4.4%. During the same timeframe, France comprised about 4% of the world's GDP and saw its voting share in the World bank drop from 4.3% to 3.8%.
>
> Which of the following can be logically concluded from the passage above?

(A)   World Bank voting shares are allocated based upon each country's share of the world's GDP.

(B)   The new ratio of voting share to percentage of world GDP is lower for China than it is for France.

(C)   Gross domestic product is the most important factor in determining voting share at the World Bank.

(D)   China should be upset that its voting share does not match its proportion of the world's GDP.

(E)   France lost some of its voting share to China because China comprised a larger portion of the world's GDP.

9.   *Barcodes*

From Chapter 7, Evidence Family

> Two-dimensional barcodes are omni-directional; that is, unlike one-dimensional barcodes, they can be scanned from any direction. Additionally, two-dimensional barcodes are smaller and can store more data than their one-dimensional counterparts. Despite such advantages, two-dimensional barcodes account for a much smaller portion of total barcode usage than one-dimensional barcodes.
>
> Which of the following, if true, most helps to resolve the apparent paradox?

(A)   Many smaller stores do not use barcodes at all because of the expense.

(B)   For some products, the amount of data necessary to be coded is small enough to fit fully on a one-dimensional barcode.

(C)   Two-dimensional barcodes are, on average, less expensive than one-dimensional barcodes.

(D)   Two-dimensional barcodes can also be scanned by consumer devices, such as cell phones.

(E)   One-dimensional barcodes last longer and are less prone to error than two-dimensional barcodes.

8

Solutions

1. Gray Wolf Population

(A) Introducing additional evidence that undermines an assumption made by the representative

This is the correct answer.

(B) Challenging the representative's definition of a critical breeding number

This answer Switches Terms. The environmentalist discusses critical breeding number, not the representative.

(C) Demonstrating that the critical breeding number of the two wolf populations differs significantly

This doesn't fit neatly into one of the standard trap categories. The environmentalist does mention the term "critical breeding number," but does not say that this number differs significantly. Rather, the environmentalist says that the population size differs.

(D) Implying that the two populations of wolves could be combined in order to preserve the species

This is a Real-World Distraction answer. It might be an interesting strategy in the real world, but the argument doesn't mention it.

(E) Suggesting that the Montana wolf population grew at a faster rate than stated in the representative's argument

This is a Switching Terms answer. The environmentalist does mention a number, but that number does not represent a rate of growth.

2. Malaria

(A) It provides support for the explanation of a particular phenomenon.

This is the correct answer.

(B) It presents evidence that contradicts an established fact.

This doesn't fit neatly into one of the standard trap categories. The boldface text does contradict what people once thought about malaria, but what they once thought was not an established fact.

(C) It offers confirmation of a contested assumption.

This is a One Word Off trap—nothing was contested in the argument.

8

(D) It identifies the cause of an erroneous conclusion.

> *This could be a Reverse Logic trap; you're looking for something that supports the conclusion.*

(E) It proposes a new conclusion in place of an earlier conjecture.

> *This is a general Diversion answer; the argument does do this in general, but not the statement in boldface.*

3. Oil and Ethanol

(A) Electric power is not a superior alternative to ethanol in supplementing automobile gasoline consumption.

> *This answer is an Irrelevant Distinction. The argument is about oil and ethanol, not electric power.*

(B) In Country N, domestic production of ethanol is increasing more quickly than domestic oil production.

> *This doesn't fit neatly into one of the standard trap categories. It looks good at first glance, but isn't actually necessary (which is a requirement for a correct answer on an Assumption question).*

(C) Ethanol is suitable for the heating of homes and other applications aside from automobiles.

> *This has No Tie to the Argument. What does the heating of homes have to do with the argument?*

(D) In Country N, gasoline consumption is not increasing at a substantially higher rate than domestic oil and ethanol production.

> *This is the correct answer.*

(E) Ethanol is as efficient as gasoline in terms of mileage per gallon when used as fuel for automobiles.

> *This answer makes an Irrelevant Distinction. Knowing how efficient the two are generally might help, but they don't necessarily have to be equally efficient.*

4. Charity

(A) Marketing efforts are only one way to solicit charitable donations.

> *This answer discusses an Irrelevant Distinction. It may be true that there are other ways to solicit donations besides marketing efforts, but the argument itself is about marketing efforts.*

8

(B) Not all impoverished families donate to charity.

> *This answer is One Word Off. It makes a statement about "all" impoverished families, but the argument never says that all of these families act in the same way. (Note: many people will eliminate this answer because the word "all" is extreme. It's true that this argument does not provide support for the extreme word "all," but extreme words can appear in correct answers—if the argument provides support for the extreme word.)*

(C) Some charitable marketing efforts are so expensive that the resulting donations fail to cover the costs of the marketing campaign.

> *This is an especially tricky No Tie to the Argument answer. The argument never talks about whether the marketing campaign will be "profitable" (that is, make more money than was spent on the marketing campaign). It might seem like this should be the goal of any charitable marketing campaign, but the argument doesn't address this.*

(D) Percentage of income is not necessarily indicative of absolute dollar value.

> *This is the correct answer.*

(E) People are more likely to donate to the same causes to which their friends donate.

> *This sounds plausible in the real world, but it's just a distraction here—the argument doesn't address this issue.*

5. Food Allergies

(A) The percentage of allergy victims who were not aware of the allergy before a major episode

> *This answer makes an Irrelevant Distinction. Knowing the exact percentage doesn't actually tell you anything.*

(B) The percentage of the population that is at risk for allergic reactions

> *This answer has No Tie to the Argument because it talks about all allergies in general, not just food allergies.*

(C) Whether some of the eight foods are common ingredients used in cooking

> *This doesn't fit neatly into one of the standard trap categories. The argument does not hinge on how commonly used the foods must be in order to warrant testing. Further, the argument does not limit itself to foods that must be cooked.*

(D) Whether an allergy to one type of food makes someone more likely to be allergic to other types of food

> *This answer makes an Irrelevant Distinction; the argument doesn't address whether someone is allergic to multiple types of food.*

(E) Whether ingesting a very small amount of an allergen is sufficient to provoke an allergic reaction in a susceptible individual

> *This is the correct answer.*

6. Smithtown Theatre

(A) A large movie chain plans to open a new multiplex location in Smithtown later this year.

> *This one can be considered either No Tie to the Argument (a different movie chain doesn't matter to this conclusion) or Reverse Logic (if anything, the new movie theatre might take some business from Smithtown Theatre, strengthening the author's claim).*

(B) Concession sales in the Smithtown Theatre comprise a substantial proportion of the theatre's revenues.

> *This one has No Tie to the Conclusion. Knowing this information about concession sales tells you nothing new about the theatre's plans to expand.*

(C) Many recent arrivals to Smithtown are students who are less likely to attend the Smithtown Theatre than are older residents.

> *This is a Reverse Logic trap because it strengthens the author's claim (and this is a Weaken question).*

(D) The expansion would allow the Smithtown Theatre to stage larger, more popular shows that will attract customers from neighboring towns.

> *This is the correct answer.*

(E) The Board of the Smithtown Theatre often solicits input from residents of the town when choosing which shows to stage.

> *This sounds good in the real world, but it really has No Tie to the Argument. Two traps for the price of one!*

8

7. Digital Coupons

(A) Computers are available for free in libraries, schools, and community centers.

> *If anything, this answer choice weakens the author's claim, and this is a Strengthen question. This is a Reverse Logic trap.*

(B) The redemption rate of ordinary coupons is particularly high among elderly and low-income people who do not know how to use computers.

> *This is the correct answer.*

(C) Many homes, including those of elderly and low-income people, do not have high-speed internet connections.

> *This argument makes an Irrelevant Distinction. The argument says nothing about having to have <u>high-speed</u> internet connections.*

(D) More homemakers than elderly people would use computers if they had access to them.

> *This answer is making an Irrelevant Distinction between two groups that are treated the same in the argument.*

(E) The redemption rate for coupons found on the internet has risen in the last five years.

> *This answer has No Tie to the Argument. The argument claims that paper coupons are in wider use because some people have difficulty accessing electronic coupons.*

8. World Bank

(A) World Bank voting shares are allocated based upon each country's share of the world's GDP.

> *This sounds as though it could be reasonable in the real world, but they didn't provide enough data points to say that this is definitely true.*

(B) The new ratio of voting share to percentage of world GDP is lower for China than it is for France.

> *This is the correct answer.*

(C) Gross domestic product is the most important factor in determining voting share at the World Bank.

> *You can think of this as an Irrelevant Comparison because it says that something is the "most important factor" when the argument doesn't actually say that at all.*

(D) China should be upset that its voting share does not match its proportion of the world's GDP.

> *This might be reasonable to believe in the real world, but the argument mentions nothing about how China "should" feel about anything.*

(E) France lost some of its voting share to China because China comprised a larger portion of the world's GDP.

> *This is a Switching Terms answer because it includes many words and terms from the argument, however, this answer imposes a cause-effect relationship that wasn't given in the argument.*

9. Barcodes

(A) Many smaller stores do not use barcodes at all because of the expense.

> *This choice makes an Irrelevant Distinction. The argument talks about stores that do use barcodes, not stores that don't.*

(B) For some products, the amount of data necessary to be coded is small enough to fit fully on a one-dimensional barcode.

> *This one is very tempting, but it's also a One Word Off trap. The choice addresses only "some" products—not enough to affect the conclusion.*

(C) Two-dimensional barcodes are, on average, less expensive than one-dimensional barcodes.

> *This is a Reverse Logic trap. If this choice were true, it would make the discrepancy even more strange, because it offers another reason why people would want to use 2D barcodes.*

(D) Two-dimensional barcodes can also be scanned by consumer devices, such as cell phones.

> *This can be considered a Reverse Logic trap (because it makes 2D barcodes more attractive) or a No Tie to the Argument trap (because scanning with consumer devices isn't part of the scope of the argument).*

(E) One-dimensional barcodes last longer and are less prone to error than two-dimensional barcodes.

> *This is the correct answer.*

8

GO BEYOND BOOKS.
TRY A FREE CLASS NOW.

IN-PERSON COURSE

Find a GMAT course near you and attend the first session free, no strings attached. You'll meet your instructor, learn how the GMAT is scored, review strategies for Data Sufficiency, dive into Sentence Correction, and gain insights into a wide array of GMAT principles and strategies.

Find your city at manhattanprep.com/gmat/classes

ONLINE COURSE

Enjoy the flexibility of prepping from home or the office with our online course. Your instructor will cover all the same content and strategies as an in-person course, while giving you the freedom to prep where you want. Attend the first session free to check out our cutting-edge online classroom.

See the full schedule at manhattanprep.com/gmat/classes

GMAT® INTERACT™

GMAT Interact is a comprehensive self-study program that is fun, intuitive, and driven by you. Each interactive video lesson is taught by an expert instructor and can be accessed on your computer or mobile device. Lessons are personalized for you based on the choices you make.

Try 5 full lessons for free at manhattanprep.com/gmat/interact

Not sure which is right for you? Try all three! Or give us a call and we'll help you figure out which program fits you best.

Toll-Free U.S. Number (800) 576-4628 | **International** 001 (212) 721-7400 | **Email** gmat@manhattanprep.com

PREP MADE PERSONAL

Whether you want quick coaching
in a particular GMAT subject area
or a comprehensive study plan developed
around your goals, we've got you covered.
Our expert, 99th percentile GMAT tutors
can help you hit your top score.

CHECK OUT THESE REVIEWS FROM MANHATTAN PREP TUTORING STUDENTS.